ALBUQUERQUE
RESTAURANT GUIDE
2020

RESTAURANTS, BARS AND CAFES
Your Guide to Authentic Regional Eats

GUIDE BOOK FOR TOURIST

ALBUQUERQUE RESTAURANT GUIDE 2020
Best Rated Restaurants in Albuquerque, New Mexico

ALBUQUERQUE RESTAURANTS 2020

The Most Recommended Restaurants in Albuquerque

This directory is dedicated to the Business Owners and Managers who provide the experience that the locals and tourists enjoy. Thanks you very much for all that you do and thank for being the "People Choice".

Thanks to everyone that posts their reviews online and the amazing reviews sites that make our life easier.

The places listed in this book are the most positively reviewed and recommended by locals and travelers from around the world.

Thank you for your time and enjoy the directory that is designed with locals and tourist in mind!

TOP 500
RESTAURANTS
Ranked from #1 to #500

#1
Guava Tree Cafe
Cuisines: Latin American,
Caribbean, Sandwiches
Average price: Modest
Area: Nob Hill
Address: 118 Richmond Dr NE
Albuquerque, NM 87106
Phone: (505) 990-2599

#2
Pollito Con Papas
Cuisines: Peruvian
Average price: Inexpensive
Area: International District
Address: 6105 Gibson SE
Albuquerque, NM 87108
Phone: (505) 765-5486

#3
Eclectic Urban Pizzeria & Tap House
Cuisines: Pizza, Wine Bar, Beer Garden
Average price: Modest
Area: Midtown/University
Address: 2119 Menaul Blvd NE
Albuquerque, NM 87107
Phone: (505) 322-2863

#4
Asian Pear
Cuisines: Japanese, Korean, Vegetarian
Average price: Inexpensive
Area: Downtown
Address: 508 Central Ave SW
Albuquerque, NM 87102
Phone: (505) 766-9405

#5
Central Grill and Coffee House
Cuisines: Coffee & Tea, Sandwiches,
Breakfast & Brunch
Average price: Inexpensive
Area: Old Town
Address: 2056 Central Ave SW
Albuquerque, NM 87104
Phone: (505) 554-1424

#6
Bocadillos Slow Roasted
Cuisines: Sandwiches
Average price: Inexpensive
Area: Midtown/University
Address: 3600 Cutler Ave NE
Albuquerque, NM 87110
Phone: (505) 910-8905

#7
Magokoro
Cuisines: Japanese
Average price: Modest
Area: Uptown
Address: 5614 Menaul Blvd NE
Albuquerque, NM 87110
Phone: (505) 830-2061

#8
The Grove Cafe & Market
Cuisines: Coffee & Tea, American
Average price: Modest
Area: Downtown
Address: 600 Central Ave SE
Albuquerque, NM 87102
Phone: (505) 248-9800

#9
El Paisa
Cuisines: Mexican
Average price: Inexpensive
Area: Barelas/South Valley
Address: 820 Bridge SW
Albuquerque, NM 87105
Phone: (505) 452-8997

#10
Taqueria Mexico
Cuisines: Mexican
Average price: Inexpensive
Area: Downtown
Address: 415 Lomas Blvd NE
Albuquerque, NM 87102
Phone: (505) 242-3445

#11
Poki Poki Cevicheria
Cuisines: Latin American,
Asian Fusion, Seafood
Average price: Modest
Area: Midtown/University
Address: 2300 Central Ave SE
Albuquerque, NM 87106
Phone: (505) 503-1077

#12
Rustic On the Green
Cuisines: American, Burgers
Average price: Modest
Area: Midtown/University
Address: 3600 Cutler Ave NE
Albuquerque, NM 87110
Phone: (505) 944-5849

#13
Pete's Frites
Cuisines: Burgers, Salad, Breakfast & Brunch
Average price: Inexpensive
Area: Nob Hill
Address: 3407 Central NE
Albuquerque, NM 87106
Phone: (505) 200-0661

#14
Banh Mi Coda
Cuisines: Sandwiches, Vietnamese
Average price: Inexpensive
Area: International District
Address: 230-C Louisiana Blvd SE
Albuquerque, NM 87108
Phone: (505) 232-0085

#15
Fork & Fig
Cuisines: Burgers, Sandwiches, Salad
Average price: Modest
Area: Uptown
Address: 6904 Menaul Blvd NE
Albuquerque, NM 87110
Phone: (505) 881-5293

#16
Ajiaco Colombian Bistro
Cuisines: Colombian
Average price: Modest
Area: Nob Hill
Address: 3216 Silver Ave SE
Albuquerque, NM 87106
Phone: (505) 266-2305

#17
The Grill On Menaul
Cuisines: American, Steakhouse, Burgers
Average price: Inexpensive
Area: Midtown/University
Address: 4615 Menaul Blvd NE
Albuquerque, NM 87110
Phone: (505) 872-9772

#18
The Last Call
Cuisines: Mexican
Average price: Inexpensive
Area: Nob Hill
Address: 102 Richmond Dr NE
Albuquerque, NM 87106
Phone: (505) 369-6102

#19
Naruto
Cuisines: Ramen, Beer Bar, Izakaya
Average price: Inexpensive
Area: Midtown/University
Address: 2110 Central Ave SE
Albuquerque, NM 87106
Phone: (505) 369-1039

#20
Antiquity Restaurant
Cuisines: Seafood, Steakhouse, Desserts
Average price: Expensive
Area: Old Town
Address: 112 Romero St NW
Albuquerque, NM 87104
Phone: (505) 247-3545

#21
Pop-Up Dumpling House
Cuisines: Szechuan, Taiwanese
Average price: Inexpensive
Area: International District
Address: 88 Louisiana Blvd SE
Albuquerque, NM 87108
Phone: (505) 268-0206

#22
Vick's Vittles
Cuisines: American,
Breakfast & Brunch, Barbeque
Average price: Inexpensive
Area: Eastside
Address: 8810 Central Ave SE
Albuquerque, NM 87123
Phone: (505) 298-5143

#23
El Cotorro
Cuisines: Mexican, Vegan, Vegetarian
Average price: Modest
Area: Nob Hill
Address: 111 Carlisle Blvd NE
Albuquerque, NM 87106
Phone: (505) 503-6202

#24
Cocina Azul
Cuisines: Mexican
Average price: Modest
Area: Downtown
Address: 1134 Mountain Rd NW
Albuquerque, NM 87102
Phone: (505) 831-2500

#25
Fu Yuang Korean & Chinese Restaurant
Cuisines: Chinese, Korean
Average price: Modest
Area: Eastside
Address: 3107 Eubank Blvd NE
Albuquerque, NM 87111
Phone: (505) 298-8989

#26
Red Rock Deli
Cuisines: German, Polish, Deli
Average price: Inexpensive
Area: Eastside
Address: 13025 Lomas Blvd NE
Albuquerque, NM 87112
Phone: (505) 332-9656

#27
Noodle King
Cuisines: Noodles, Vietnamese
Average price: Inexpensive
Area: Downtown
Address: 109 Gold Ave SW
Albuquerque, NM 87102
Phone: (505) 503-8491

#28
Nexus Brewery
Cuisines: Brewery, Soul Food, Southern
Average price: Modest
Area: Business Parkway/Academy Acres
Address: 4730 Pan American E Fwy NE
Albuquerque, NM 87109
Phone: (505) 242-4100

#29
Bistronomy B2B
Cuisines: Burgers, Bar, Brewery
Average price: Modest
Area: Nob Hill
Address: 3118 Central Ave SE
Albuquerque, NM 87106
Phone: (505) 262-2222

#30
Crackin' Crab
Cuisines: Seafood
Average price: Modest
Area: Business Parkway/Academy Acres
Address: 4959 Pan America Fwy NE
Albuquerque, NM 87109
Phone: (505) 344-4469

#31
Tsai's Chinese Bistro
Cuisines: Taiwanese, Chinese
Average price: Modest
Area: Uptown
Address: 2325 San Pedro Dr NE
Albuquerque, NM 87110
Phone: (505) 508-2925

#33
Tia Betty Blue's
Cuisines: Breakfast & Brunch
Average price: Inexpensive
Area: International District
Address: 1248 San Mateo SE
Albuquerque, NM 87108
Phone: (505) 268-1955

#32
Curry Leaf
Cuisines: Indian
Average price: Modest
Area: Business Parkway/Academy Acres
Address: 6910 Montgomery Blvd NE
Albuquerque, NM 87109
Phone: (505) 881-3663

#34
The Range Café
Cuisines: Breakfast & Brunch, Diner, Desserts
Average price: Modest
Area: Midtown/University
Address: 2200 Menaul NE
Albuquerque, NM 87107
Phone: (505) 888-1660

#35
Le Troquet
Cuisines: French, Salad, Sandwiches
Average price: Modest
Area: Downtown
Address: 228 Gold St SW
Albuquerque, NM 87102
Phone: (505) 508-1166

#36
El Modelo Mexican Foods
Cuisines: Mexican
Average price: Inexpensive
Area: Barelas/South Valley
Address: 1715 2nd St SW
Albuquerque, NM 87102
Phone: (505) 242-1843

#37
Richie Bs Pizza
Cuisines: Pizza, Sandwiches, Italian
Average price: Inexpensive
Area: Business Parkway/Academy Acres
Address: 7200 Montgomery Blvd NE
Albuquerque, NM 87109
Phone: (505) 312-8579

#38
Sharky's
Cuisines: Mexican
Average price: Inexpensive
Area: Barelas/South Valley
Address: 5420 Central Ave SW
Álbuquerque, NM 87105
Phone: (505) 831-8905

#39
ZS & T's
Cuisines: American, Mexican
Average price: Inexpensive
Area: Midtown/University
Address: 5017 Menaul Blvd NE
Albuquerque, NM 87110
Phone: (505) 200-0065

#40
Vinaigrette
Cuisines: Salad, American
Average price: Modest
Area: Old Town
Address: 1828 Central Ave SW
Albuquerque, NM 87104
Phone: (505) 842-5507

#41
The Cellar Tapas Beer and Wine
Cuisines: Tapas/Small Plates, Wine Bar
Average price: Modest
Area: Downtown
Address: 1025 Lomas Blvd NW
Albuquerque, NM 87102
Phone: (505) 242-3117

#42
Aura European
Mediterranean Restaurant
Cuisines: Mediterranean, Armenian
Average price: Modest
Area: Business Parkway/Academy Acres
Address: 6300 San Mateo Blvd NE
Albuquerque, NM 87109
Phone: (505) 508-3224

#43
Ben Michael's Restaurant
Cuisines: Wine Bar, Coffee & Tea, Mexican
Average price: Modest
Area: Old Town
Address: 2404 Pueblo Bonito Ct NW
Albuquerque, NM 87104
Phone: (505) 224-2817

#44
Namaste
Cuisines: Indian, Himalayan/Nepalese
Average price: Modest
Area: Midtown/University
Address: 110 Yale Blvd SE
Albuquerque, NM 87106
Phone: (505) 266-6900

#45
Mary & Tito's Cafe
Cuisines: Mexican, Mexican
Average price: Inexpensive
Area: North Valley/Los Ranchos
Address: 2711 4th St NW
Albuquerque, NM 87107
Phone: (505) 344-6266

#46
Canteen Brewhouse
Cuisines: Gastropub, Brewery
Average price: Inexpensive
Area: Business Parkway/Academy Acres
Address: 2381 Aztec Rd
Albuquerque, NM 87107
Phone: (505) 881-2737

#47
The Grain Station
Cuisines: Pub, German, American
Average price: Inexpensive
Area: Midtown/University
Address: 2004 Central Ave SE
Albuquerque, NM 87106
Phone: (505) 242-4992

#48
Karibu Café
Cuisines: African, Caribbean
Average price: Modest
Area: Eastside
Address: 3107 Eubank Blvd NE
Albuquerque, NM 87111
Phone: (505) 275-4981

#49
Peppers Ole Fashion BBQ
Cuisines: Barbeque
Average price: Modest
Area: International District
Address: 303 San Pedro Dr NE
Albuquerque, NM 87108
Phone: (505) 967-6427

#50
Saigon Far East
Cuisines: Vietnamese
Average price: Inexpensive
Area: International District
Address: 901 San Pedro Dr SE
Albuquerque, NM 87108
Phone: (505) 255-7408

#51
Golden Crown Panaderia
Cuisines: Bakery, Coffee & Tea, Pizza
Average price: Inexpensive
Area: Downtown
Address: 1103 Mountain Rd NW
Albuquerque, NM 87102
Phone: (505) 243-2424

#52
Thai Heritage Restaurant
Cuisines: Thai, Desserts
Average price: Modest
Area: Business Parkway/Academy Acres
Address: 6219 Montgomery Blvd NE
Albuquerque, NM 87109
Phone: (505) 883-3989

#53
Pho 79
Cuisines: Vietnamese
Average price: Inexpensive
Area: Business Parkway/Academy Acres
Address: 2007 Candalaria Rd NE
Albuquerque, NM 87107
Phone: (505) 883-3747

#54
El Patio De Albuquerque
Cuisines: Mexican
Average price: Modest
Area: Midtown/University
Address: 142 Harvard Dr SE
Albuquerque, NM 87106
Phone: (505) 268-4245

#55
The Crown Room
Cuisines: American, Steakhouse
Average price: Exclusive
Area: Nob Hill
Address: 145 Louisiana Blvd NE
Albuquerque, NM 87108
Phone: (505) 767-7180

#56
O Ramen
Cuisines: Ramen
Average price: Inexpensive
Area: Midtown/University
Address: 2114 Central Ave
Albuquerque, NM 87106
Phone: (505) 508-1897

#57
Elaine's
Cuisines: American
Average price: Expensive
Area: Nob Hill
Address: 3503 Central Ave
Albuquerque, NM 87106
Phone: (505) 433-4782

#58
Tacos Mex Y Mariscos
Cuisines: Mexican
Average price: Inexpensive
Area: North Valley/Los Ranchos
Address: 5201 4th St NW
Albuquerque, NM 87107
Phone: (505) 344-1466

#59
Al's Big Dipper
Cuisines: Fast Food, Sandwiches, Soup
Average price: Inexpensive
Area: Downtown
Address: 501 Copper Ave NW
Albuquerque, NM 87102
Phone: (505) 314-1118

#60
Cecilia's Cafe
Cuisines: Mexican
Average price: Inexpensive
Area: Downtown
Address: 230 6th St SW
Albuquerque, NM 87102
Phone: (505) 243-7070

#61
Frank's Famous Chicken & Waffles
Cuisines: Soul Food, Chicken Shop, Waffles
Average price: Modest
Area: Midtown/University
Address: 513 San Mateo Blvd NE
Albuquerque, NM 87108
Phone: (505) 712-5109

#62
Cafe Lush
Cuisines: American
Average price: Modest
Area: Downtown
Address: 700 Tijeras Ave NW
Albuquerque, NM 87102
Phone: (505) 508-0164

#63
The Artichoke Cafe
Cuisines: American, Cafe
Average price: Expensive
Area: Downtown
Address: 424 Central Ave SE
Albuquerque, NM 87102
Phone: (505) 243-0200

#64
Firenze Pizzeria
Cuisines: Pizza
Average price: Modest
Area: Downtown
Address: 900 Park Ave SW
Albuquerque, NM 87102
Phone: (505) 242-2939

#65
Padilla's Mexican Kitchen
Cuisines: Mexican
Average price: Inexpensive
Area: Midtown/University
Address: 1510 Girard Blvd NE
Albuquerque, NM 87106
Phone: (505) 262-0115

#66
Havana Restaurant
Cuisines: Cuban, Sandwiches
Average price: Modest
Area: Uptown
Address: 5331 Menaul Blvd NE
Albuquerque, NM 87110
Phone: (505) 830-2025

#67
Leilani's Café
Cuisines: American, Mexican
Average price: Inexpensive
Area: International District
Address: 5901 Gibson Blvd SE
Albuquerque, NM 87108
Phone: (505) 349-8820

#68
Eli's Place
Cuisines: Mexican, Mexican,
Breakfast & Brunch
Average price: Modest
Area: North Valley/Los Ranchos
Address: 6313 4th St NW
Albuquerque, NM 87107
Phone: (505) 345-3935

#69
Zohra Authentic Foods
Cuisines: Diner, Cafe, Greek
Average price: Inexpensive
Area: Downtown
Address: 20 First Plz NW
Albuquerque, NM 87102
Phone: (505) 247-2323

#70
La Salita Restaurant
Cuisines: Mexican
Average price: Modest
Area: Eastside
Address: 1217 Eubank Blvd NE
Albuquerque, NM 87112
Phone: (505) 299-9968

#71
La Mexicana
Cuisines: Mexican
Average price: Inexpensive
Area: Barelas/South Valley
Address: 304 Coal Ave SW
Albuquerque, NM 87102
Phone: (505) 242-2558

#72
Cervantes Restaurant & Lounge
Cuisines: Mexican, Lounge
Average price: Modest
Area: International District
Address: 5801 Gibson Blvd SE
Albuquerque, NM 87108
Phone: (505) 262-2253

#73
N'awlins Mardi Gras Cafe
Cuisines: Cajun/Creole, Seafood, Southern
Average price: Modest
Area: Nob Hill
Address: 3718 Central Ave SE
Albuquerque, NM 87108
Phone: (505) 200-9600

#74
Yasmine's Cafe
Cuisines: Middle Eastern, Greek,
Mediterranean
Average price: Inexpensive
Area: Midtown/University
Address: 1600 Central Ave SE
Albuquerque, NM 87106
Phone: (505) 242-1980

#75
Frontier Restaurant
Cuisines: Mexican, Diner, American
Average price: Inexpensive
Area: Midtown/University
Address: 2400 Central Ave SE
Albuquerque, NM 87106
Phone: (505) 266-0550

#76
Pad Thai Cafe
Cuisines: Thai, Desserts, American
Average price: Inexpensive
Area: International District
Address: 110 Louisiana Blvd SE
Albuquerque, NM 87108
Phone: (505) 266-0567

#77
Down N Dirty Seafood Boil
Cuisines: Seafood
Average price: Modest
Area: Business Parkway/Academy Acres
Address: 6100 4th St NW
Albuquerque, NM 87107
Phone: (505) 345-0595

#78
Amore Neapolitan Pizzeria
Cuisines: Pizza, Italian
Average price: Modest
Area: Midtown/University
Address: 3600 Cutler Ave NE
Albuquerque, NM 87110
Phone: (505) 554-1967

#79
Canvas Artistry
Cuisines: American
Average price: Modest
Area: Nob Hill
Address: 3120 Central Ave SE
Albuquerque, NM 87106
Phone: (505) 639-5214

#80
Monroe's Restaurant
Cuisines: Mexican, Latin American
Average price: Modest
Area: Old Town
Address: 1520 Lomas Blvd NW
Albuquerque, NM 87104
Phone: (505) 242-1111

#81
Down N Dirty Seafood Boil
Cuisines: Seafood
Average price: Modest
Area: Eastside
Address: 4200 Wyoming Blvd NE
Albuquerque, NM 87111
Phone: (505) 639-4758

#82
99 Degrees Seafood Kitchen
Cuisines: Cajun/Creole, Seafood, Desserts
Average price: Modest
Area: Nob Hill
Address: 3409 Central Ave NE
Albuquerque, NM 87106
Phone: (505) 433-4929

#83
Tucanos Brazilian Grill
Cuisines: Brazilian, Seafood, Steakhouse
Average price: Modest
Area: Downtown
Address: 110 Central Ave SW
Albuquerque, NM 87102
Phone: (505) 246-9900

#84
Two Fools Tavern
Cuisines: Irish, Irish Pub
Average price: Modest
Area: Nob Hill
Address: 3211 Central Ave NE
Albuquerque, NM 87106
Phone: (505) 265-7447

#85
M'Tucci's Italian Market & Deli
Cuisines: Deli, Meat Shop, Sandwiches
Average price: Modest
Area: North Valley/Los Ranchos
Address: 6001 Winter Haven Rd NW
Albuquerque, NM 87120
Phone: (505) 639-4819

#86
Roma Bakery and Deli
Cuisines: Deli, Salad, Sandwiches
Average price: Inexpensive
Area: Downtown
Address: 501 Roma Ave NW
Albuquerque, NM 87102
Phone: (505) 843-9418

#87
Chumlys Southwestern
Cuisines: Hot Dogs, Soup, Mexican
Average price: Inexpensive
Area: Midtown/University
Address: 3600 Cutler Ave NE
Albuquerque, NM 87110
Phone: (505) 401-5827

#88
Perea's New Mexican Restaurant
Cuisines: Mexican
Average price: Inexpensive
Area: Eastside
Address: 1140 Juan Tabo Blvd NE
Albuquerque, NM 87123
Phone: (505) 293-0157

#89
Kabob House
Cuisines: Middle Eastern, Persian/Iranian
Average price: Modest
Area: Airport/Base
Address: 301 Cornell Dr SE
Albuquerque, NM 87106
Phone: (505) 312-8949

#90
Standard Diner
Cuisines: Diner, Burgers, American
Average price: Modest
Area: Downtown
Address: 320 Central Ave SE
Albuquerque, NM 87102
Phone: (505) 243-1440

#91
Filling Philly's
Cuisines: American, Deli, Sandwiches
Average price: Modest
Area: Uptown
Address: 6904 Menaul Blvd NE
Albuquerque, NM 87110
Phone: (505) 830-4444

#92
Anatolia Turkish Mediterranean Grill
Cuisines: Mediterranean, Turkish
Average price: Modest
Area: Downtown
Address: 313 B Central Ave NW
Albuquerque, NM 87102
Phone: (505) 242-6718

#93
Sahara Middle Eastern Eatery
Cuisines: Middle Eastern, Mediterranean,
Vegetarian
Average price: Inexpensive
Area: Midtown/University
Address: 2622 Central Ave SE
Albuquerque, NM 87106
Phone: (505) 255-5400

#94
Bangkok Bite
Cuisines: Thai, Tea Room
Average price: Inexpensive
Area: Uptown
Address: 8246 Menaul Blvd NE
Albuquerque, NM 87110
Phone: (505) 219-3831

#95
35 Degree North Coffee
Cuisines: Breakfast & Brunch
Average price: Inexpensive
Area: Old Town
Address: 1720 Central Ave SW
Albuquerque, NM 87104
Phone: (505) 243-6495

#96
**Bucket Headz Southern
Home Cooking**
Cuisines: Southern, Soul Food, Buffet
Average price: Modest
Area: International District
Address: 1218 San Pedro SE
Albuquerque, NM 87108
Phone: (505) 268-7685

#97
Farina Pizzeria & Wine Bar
Cuisines: Pizza, Italian, Wine Bar
Average price: Modest
Area: Downtown
Address: 510 Central Ave SE
Albuquerque, NM 87102
Phone: (505) 243-0130

#98
Fan Tang
Cuisines: Chinese
Average price: Modest
Area: Nob Hill
Address: 3523 Central Ave NE
Albuquerque, NM 87106
Phone: (505) 266-3566

#99
Rising Star Chinese Eatery
Cuisines: Chinese
Average price: Inexpensive
Area: Business Parkway/Academy Acres
Address: 7001 San Antonio Dr NE
Albuquerque, NM 87109
Phone: (505) 821-6595

#100
Fareast Fuzion
Cuisines: Sushi Bar, Chinese, Asian Fusion
Average price: Modest
Area: International District
Address: 5901 Central Ave NE
Albuquerque, NM 87108
Phone: (505) 255-2910

#101
San Pedro Middle East Restaurant
Cuisines: Middle Eastern
Average price: Inexpensive
Area: Business Parkway/Academy Acres
Address: 4001 San Pedro Dr NE
Albuquerque, NM 87110
Phone: (505) 888-2921

#102
Tia B's La Waffleria
Cuisines: Breakfast & Brunch, Coffee & Tea
Average price: Modest
Area: Nob Hill
Address: 3710 Campus Blvd NE
Albuquerque, NM 87106
Phone: (505) 492-2007

#103
The Shop
Cuisines: Breakfast & Brunch
Average price: Modest
Area: Nob Hill
Address: 2933 Monte Vista Blvd Ne
Albuquerque, NM 87106
Phone: (505) 433-2795

#104
The Cube
Cuisines: American, Barbeque, Hot Dogs
Average price: Modest
Area: Midtown/University
Address: 1520 Central Ave SE
Albuquerque, NM 87106
Phone: (505) 243-0023

#105
Model Pharmacy
Cuisines: DrugStore, Cafe, American
Average price: Modest
Area: Nob Hill
Address: 3636 Monte Vista Blvd NE
Albuquerque, NM 87106
Phone: (505) 255-8686

#106
Mac's La Sierra Restaurant
Cuisines: Mexican, Seafood, Steakhouse
Average price: Inexpensive
Area: Westside
Address: 6217 Central Ave NW
Albuquerque, NM 87105
Phone: (505) 836-1212

#107
Mak's QuickFire Kitchen
Cuisines: Chinese, Soup
Average price: Inexpensive
Area: Downtown
Address: 411 Central Ave NW
Albuquerque, NM 87102
Phone: (505) 242-6563

#108
Acapulco Tacos & Burritos
Cuisines: Mexican
Average price: Inexpensive
Area: International District
Address: 840 San Mateo Blvd SE
Albuquerque, NM 87108
Phone: (505) 268-9865

#109
Farm & Table
Cuisines: American, Breakfast & Brunch
Average price: Modest
Area: North Valley/Los Ranchos
Address: 8917 4th St NW
Albuquerque, NM 87114
Phone: (505) 503-7124

#110
High Noon Restaurant & Saloon
Cuisines: Steakhouse
Average price: Modest
Area: Old Town
Address: 425 San Felipe Rd NW
Albuquerque, NM 87104
Phone: (505) 765-1455

#111
Zinc Wine Bar & Bistro
Cuisines: American, Bar, Music Venue
Average price: Modest
Area: Nob Hill
Address: 3009 Central Ave NE
Albuquerque, NM 87106
Phone: (505) 254-9462

#112
Holy Cow
Cuisines: Burgers
Average price: Modest
Area: Downtown
Address: 700 Central SE
Albuquerque, NM 87102
Phone: (505) 242-2991

#113
Los Compadres Restaurant
Cuisines: Mexican, Burgers
Average price: Inexpensive
Area: Old Town
Address: 2437 Central Ave NW
Albuquerque, NM 87104
Phone: (505) 452-8091

#114
Sadie's Of New Mexico
Cuisines: Mexican
Average price: Modest
Area: Business Parkway/Academy Acres
Address: 6230 4th St NW
Albuquerque, NM 87107
Phone: (505) 345-5339

#115
Java Joe's
Cuisines: Coffee & Tea, Cafe
Average price: Inexpensive
Area: Downtown
Address: 906 Park Ave SW
Albuquerque, NM 87102
Phone: (505) 765-1514

#116
Basil Leaf Vietnamese Restaurant
Cuisines: Vietnamese
Average price: Modest
Area: Eastside
Address: 1225 Eubank NE
Albuquerque, NM 87112
Phone: (505) 323-2594

#117
Sister
Cuisines: Bar, Music Venue, Mexican
Average price: Modest
Area: Downtown
Address: 407 Central Ave NW
Albuquerque, NM 87102
Phone: (505) 242-4900

#118
Ikrave Cafe
Cuisines: Vietnamese, Coffee & Tea, Cafe
Average price: Inexpensive
Area: Eastside
Address: 1331 Juan Tabo Blvd NE
Albuquerque, NM 87112
Phone: (505) 275-6626

#119
Sushi Xuan Asian Grill
Cuisines: Sushi Bar
Average price: Modest
Area: Eastside
Address: 417 Tramway Blvd NE
Albuquerque, NM 87123
Phone: (505) 200-2477

#120
Lollie's New Mexican Food
Cuisines: Mexican
Average price: Inexpensive
Area: Barelas/South Valley
Address: 424 Isleta Blvd SW
Albuquerque, NM 87105
Phone: (505) 452-9096

#121
Papa Frank's
Cuisines: Mexican
Average price: Inexpensive
Area: Downtown
Address: 218 Marble Ave NW
Albuquerque, NM 87102
Phone: (505) 842-8944

#122
Jimmy's Cafe On Jefferson
Cuisines: Breakfast & Brunch
Average price: Inexpensive
Area: Business Parkway/Academy Acres
Address: 7007 Jefferson St NE
Albuquerque, NM 87109
Phone: (505) 341-2546

#123
Papa Nachos
Cuisines: Mexican
Average price: Inexpensive
Area: Business Parkway/Academy Acres
Address: 7648 Louisiana Blvd NE
Albuquerque, NM 87109
Phone: (505) 821-4900

#124
Crepe Crepe
Cuisines: Desserts, French,
Breakfast & Brunch
Average price: Inexpensive
Area: Eastside
Address: 3005 Eubank Blvd NE
Albuquerque, NM 87111
Phone: (505) 323-3817

#125
Breve Crepes and Coffee
Cuisines: Creperie, Coffee & Tea
Average price: Inexpensive
Area: Downtown
Address: 400 Gold Ave SW
Albuquerque, NM 87102
Phone: (505) 243-9298

#126
Matanza Beer Kitchen
Cuisines: Mexican, Salad, Bar
Average price: Modest
Area: Nob Hill
Address: 3225 Central Ave NE
Albuquerque, NM 87106
Phone: (505) 312-7305

#127
Cafe Istanbul
Cuisines: Middle Eastern,
Turkish, Sandwiches
Average price: Inexpensive
Area: Uptown
Address: 1415 Wyoming Blvd NE
Albuquerque, NM 87112
Phone: (505) 294-9900

#128
Rudy's Country Store & BBQ
Cuisines: Barbeque
Average price: Modest
Area: Midtown/University
Address: 2321 Carlisle Blvd NE
Albuquerque, NM 87110
Phone: (505) 884-4000

#129
M'Tucci's Italian
Cuisines: Italian, Pizza
Average price: Modest
Area: North Valley/Los Ranchos
Address: 6001 Winter Haven Rd NW
Albuquerque, NM 87120
Phone: (505) 503-7327

#130
Mixx Food Bar
Cuisines: American, Beer Bar
Average price: Modest
Area: Downtown
Address: 901 Park Ave
Albuquerque, NM 87102
Phone: (505) 312-7394

#131
The Owl Cafe
Cuisines: Diner, American
Average price: Inexpensive
Area: Eastside
Address: 800 Eubank Blvd NE
Albuquerque, NM 87123
Phone: (505) 291-4900

#132
Rancher's Club of New Mexico
Cuisines: Steakhouse, Seafood
Average price: Expensive
Area: Midtown/University
Address: 1901 University Blvd. N.E.
Albuquerque, NM 87102
Phone: (505) 889-8071

#133
Lindo Mexico
Cuisines: Mexican
Average price: Modest
Area: International District
Address: 7209 Central Ave NE
Albuquerque, NM 87108
Phone: (505) 266-2999

#134
Vic's Daily Cafe
Cuisines: American, Breakfast & Brunch
Average price: Inexpensive
Area: Business Parkway/Academy Acres
Address: 3600 Osuna Rd NE
Albuquerque, NM 87109
Phone: (505) 341-9710

#135
Giovanni's Pizzeria
Cuisines: Pizza
Average price: Inexpensive
Area: International District
Address: 921 San Pedro Dr SE
Albuquerque, NM 87108
Phone: (505) 255-1233

#136
Nagomi Restaurant
Cuisines: Japanese, Sushi Bar, Hot Pot
Average price: Modest
Area: Eastside
Address: 2400 Juan Tabo Blvd NE
Albuquerque, NM 87112
Phone: (505) 298-3081

#137
Seasons Rotisserie & Grill
Cuisines: American
Average price: Modest
Area: Old Town
Address: 2031 Mountain Rd NW
Albuquerque, NM 87104
Phone: (505) 766-5100

#138
Rock & Brews - Albuquerque
Cuisines: American, Burgers, Beer Bar
Average price: Modest
Area: Business Parkway/Academy Acres
Address: 4800 Montgomery Blvd
Albuquerque, NM 87109
Phone: (505) 340-2953

#139
B2B2 Tap Room
Cuisines: Mexican, Beer Bar
Average price: Inexpensive
Area: Uptown
Address: 2201 Louisiana Blvd NE
Albuquerque, NM 87110
Phone: (505) 508-4406

#140
Kasey's
Cuisines: American, Steakhouse, Burgers
Average price: Modest
Area: Midtown/University
Address: 400 Washington SE
Albuquerque, NM 87108
Phone: (505) 241-3801

#141
Casa Taco
Cuisines: Mexican
Average price: Inexpensive
Area: Business Parkway/Academy Acres
Address: 5801 Academy Rd NE
Albuquerque, NM 87109
Phone: (505) 821-8226

#142
Weck's
Cuisines: Breakfast & Brunch
Average price: Inexpensive
Area: Downtown
Address: 2039 4th St NW
Albuquerque, NM 87102
Phone: (505) 242-1226

#143
Torinos' @ Home
Cuisines: Italian
Average price: Modest
Area: Business Parkway/Academy Acres
Address: 7600 Jefferson St NE
Albuquerque, NM 87109
Phone: (505) 797-4491

#144
India Grill
Cuisines: Indian
Average price: Modest
Area: Business Parkway/Academy Acres
Address: 6501 B Wyoming Blvd NE
Albuquerque, NM 87109
Phone: (505) 797-4243

#145
Cheddar's Scratch Kitchen
Cuisines: American, Comfort Food
Average price: Modest
Area: Business Parkway/Academy Acres
Address: 4865 Pan American W Fwy
Albuquerque, NM 87109
Phone: (505) 345-0829

#146
Cheese & Coffee Cafe Downtown
Cuisines: Cafe, Sandwiches, Salad
Average price: Inexpensive
Area: Old Town
Address: 119 San Pasquale Ave SW
Albuquerque, NM 87104
Phone: (505) 242-0326

#147
Burrito Lady
Cuisines: Mexican
Average price: Inexpensive
Area: Eastside
Address: 938 Eubank Blvd NE
Albuquerque, NM 87112
Phone: (505) 271-2268

#148
Monica's El Portal Restaurant
Cuisines: Mexican
Average price: Inexpensive
Area: Old Town
Address: 321 Rio Grande Blvd NW
Albuquerque, NM 87104
Phone: (505) 247-9625

#149
Zacatecas
Cuisines: Mexican, Bar
Average price: Modest
Area: Nob Hill
Address: 3423 Central Ave NE
Albuquerque, NM 87106
Phone: (505) 255-8226

#150
Pho Nguyen
Cuisines: Vietnamese
Average price: Inexpensive
Area: Uptown
Address: 7202 Menaul Blvd NE
Albuquerque, NM 87110
Phone: (505) 830-6554

#151
Church Street Café
Cuisines: Mexican, Bar
Average price: Modest
Area: Old Town
Address: 2111 Church St NW
Albuquerque, NM 87104
Phone: (505) 247-8522

#152
Tully's Italian Deli
Cuisines: Italian, Meat Shop, Deli
Average price: Modest
Area: Midtown/University
Address: 1425 San Mateo Blvd NE
Albuquerque, NM 87110
Phone: (505) 255-5370

#153
Thai Spice
Cuisines: Thai
Average price: Modest
Area: Business Parkway/Academy Acres
Address: 7441 Paseo Del Norte Blvd NE
Albuquerque, NM 87113
Phone: (505) 503-1521

#154
Mariscos Altamar
Cuisines: Mexican, Seafood
Average price: Modest
Area: Westside
Address: 1517 Coors Blvd NW
Albuquerque, NM 87121
Phone: (505) 831-1496

#155
Duran Central Pharmacy
Cuisines: DrugStore, Mexican, Diner
Average price: Inexpensive
Area: Old Town
Address: 1815 Central Ave NW
Albuquerque, NM 87104
Phone: (505) 247-4141

#156
Sticky Rice
Cuisines: Laotian
Average price: Inexpensive
Area: Business Parkway/Academy Acres
Address: 7600 Jefferson St NE
Albuquerque, NM 87109
Phone: (505) 797-1288

#157
Santiago's New Mexican Grill
Cuisines: Mexican
Average price: Inexpensive
Area: Eastside
Address: 1911 Eubank Blvd NE
Albuquerque, NM 87112
Phone: (505) 292-8226

#158
Savory Fare Cafe, Bakery & Catering
Cuisines: Cafe, Bakery, Caterer
Average price: Modest
Area: Business Parkway/Academy Acres
Address: 7400 Montgomery Blvd NE
Albuquerque, NM 87109
Phone: (505) 884-8514

#159
Hurricane's Restaurant & Drive-In
Cuisines: Mexican
Average price: Inexpensive
Area: Nob Hill
Address: 4330 Lomas Blvd NE
Albuquerque, NM 87110
Phone: (505) 255-4248

#160
Sadie's
Cuisines: Mexican
Average price: Modest
Area: Eastside
Address: 15 Hotel Cir NE
Albuquerque, NM 87123
Phone: (505) 296-6940

#161
El Sabor De Juarez
Cuisines: Mexican
Average price: Inexpensive
Area: Airport/Base
Address: 3527 Gibson Blvd SE
Albuquerque, NM 87106
Phone: (505) 265-3338

#162
Pappadeaux Seafood Kitchen
Cuisines: Seafood, Sports Bar
Average price: Modest
Area: Business Parkway/Academy Acres
Address: 5011 Pan American Frwy NE
Albuquerque, NM 87109
Phone: (505) 345-0240

#163
Farina Alto
Cuisines: Pizza, Italian, Wine Bar
Average price: Modest
Area: Eastside
Address: 10721 Montgomery Blvd NE
Albuquerque, NM 87111
Phone: (505) 298-0035

#164
Pueblo Harvest Cafe
Cuisines: Cafe, American
Average price: Modest
Area: North Valley/Los Ranchos
Address: 2401 12th St NW
Albuquerque, NM 87104
Phone: (505) 724-3510

#165
Il Vicino Wood Oven Pizza
Cuisines: Pizza
Average price: Modest
Area: Nob Hill
Address: 3403 Central Ave NE
Albuquerque, NM 87106
Phone: (505) 266-7855

#166
StreetFood Asia
Cuisines: Asian Fusion, Malaysian
Average price: Modest
Area: Nob Hill
Address: 3422 Central Ave SE
Albuquerque, NM 87106
Phone: (505) 260-0088

#167
Slate Street Cafe
Cuisines: American, Wine Bar
Average price: Modest
Area: Downtown
Address: 515 Slate Ave NW
Albuquerque, NM 87102
Phone: (505) 243-2210

#168
Moni's Cafe
Cuisines: Cafe
Average price: Inexpensive
Area: Barelas/South Valley
Address: 1100 Coors Blvd SW
Albuquerque, NM 87121
Phone: (505) 508-5477

#169
Piatanzi
Cuisines: Italian, Gluten-Free
Average price: Modest
Area: Midtown/University
Address: 1403 Girard Blvd NE
Albuquerque, NM 87106
Phone: (505) 792-1700

#170
Little Red Hamburger Hut
Cuisines: Burgers, Fast Food, American
Average price: Modest
Area: Old Town
Address: 15th St NW At Mountain Rd NW
Albuquerque, NM 87104
Phone: (505) 304-1819

#171
El Papaturro Restaurant
Cuisines: Salvadoran
Average price: Inexpensive
Area: North Valley/Los Ranchos
Address: 6601 4th Street NW
Albuquerque, NM 87107
Phone: (505) 503-1575

#172
The Boiler Monkey Bistro
Cuisines: Coffee & Tea, Creperie
Average price: Inexpensive
Area: Downtown
Address: 6TH And Central
Albuquerque, NM 87102
Phone: (505) 315-0567

#173
Oak Tree Cafe
Cuisines: Bar, American, Fast Food
Average price: Inexpensive
Area: Business Parkway/Academy Acres
Address: 4545 Alameda Blvd NE
Albuquerque, NM 87113
Phone: (505) 830-2233

#174
Café Laurel
Cuisines: Coffee & Tea, Sandwiches
Average price: Inexpensive
Area: Downtown
Address: 1433 Central Ave NW
Albuquerque, NM 87104
Phone: (505) 259-2331

#175
Monte Carlo Steak House
Cuisines: Steakhouse
Average price: Modest
Area: Barelas/South Valley
Address: 3916 Central Ave SW
Albuquerque, NM 87105
Phone: (505) 836-9886

#176
Mariscos La Playa
Cuisines: Seafood, Mexican
Average price: Modest
Area: Business Parkway/Academy Acres
Address: 5210 San Mateo Blvd NE
Albuquerque, NM 87109
Phone: (505) 884-1147

#177
Chinshan
Cuisines: Chinese
Average price: Modest
Area: North Valley/Los Ranchos
Address: 9780 Coors NW
Albuquerque, NM 87114
Phone: (505) 899-4578

#178
California Pastrami
Cuisines: Sandwiches, Burgers, Deli
Average price: Modest
Area: Business Parkway/Academy Acres
Address: 6125 Montgomery Blvd NE
Albuquerque, NM 87109
Phone: (505) 872-9253

#179
Gyros Mediterranean
Cuisines: Greek, Mediterranean
Average price: Inexpensive
Area: Midtown/University
Address: 106 Cornell Dr SE
Albuquerque, NM 87106
Phone: (505) 255-4401

#180
Mr Pho
Cuisines: Vietnamese
Average price: Inexpensive
Area: Business Parkway/Academy Acres
Address: 6205 Montgomery Blvd
Albuquerque, NM 87109
Phone: (505) 872-2311

#181
Asian Noodle Bar
Cuisines: Thai, Noodles
Average price: Modest
Area: Downtown
Address: 318 Central Ave SW
Albuquerque, NM 87165
Phone: (505) 224-9119

#182
Am Spices of India
Cuisines: Indian, Vegetarian, Buffet
Average price: Modest
Area: Downtown
Address: 317 Central Ave NW
Albuquerque, NM 87102
Phone: (505) 492-3570

#183
Rockin' Taco
Cuisines: Latin American, Mexican
Average price: Inexpensive
Area: Midtown/University
Address: 3600 Cutler Ave NE
Albuquerque, NM 87110
Phone: (505) 261-7541

#184
Delish
Cuisines: American
Average price: Modest
Area: North Valley/Los Ranchos
Address: 3705 Ellison Rd NW
Albuquerque, NM 87114
Phone: (505) 899-0197

#185
Cheba Hut
Cuisines: Sandwiches
Average price: Inexpensive
Area: Midtown/University
Address: 115 Harvard St
Albuquerque, NM 87106
Phone: (505) 232-2432

#186
Mannie's Family Restaurant
Cuisines: Sandwiches, Diner
Average price: Inexpensive
Area: Nob Hill
Address: 2900 Central Ave SE
Albuquerque, NM 87106
Phone: (505) 265-1669

#187
Huong Thao
Cuisines: Vietnamese
Average price: Inexpensive
Area: Eastside
Address: 1016 Juan Tabo Blvd NE
Albuquerque, NM 87112
Phone: (505) 292-8222

#188
The Ivy Tea Room
Cuisines: Cafe, Tea Room
Average price: Modest
Area: North Valley/Los Ranchos
Address: 7015 4th St NW
Albuquerque, NM 87107
Phone: (505) 345-1784

#189
The Egg & I
Cuisines: Breakfast & Brunch, Cafe, American
Average price: Modest
Area: Uptown
Address: 6909 Menaul Blvd NE
Albuquerque, NM 87110
Phone: (505) 888-3447

#190
5 Star Burger at Country Club Plaza
Cuisines: Burgers, American
Average price: Modest
Area: Old Town
Address: 1710 Central Ave SW
Albuquerque, NM 87104
Phone: (505) 764-3000

#191
Flamez Bistro
Cuisines: Burgers, American, Sandwiches
Average price: Modest
Area: Eastside
Address: 9821 Montgomery NE
Albuquerque, NM 87111
Phone: (505) 275-0522

#192
Garduño's at Old Town
Cuisines: Mexican, Bar
Average price: Modest
Area: Old Town
Address: 800 Rio Grande Blvd NW
Albuquerque, NM 87104
Phone: (505) 222-8766

#193
K & I Diner
Cuisines: Mexican
Average price: Inexpensive
Area: Barelas/South Valley
Address: 2500 Broadway Blvd SE
Albuquerque, NM 87102
Phone: (505) 243-1881

#194
Kap's Coffee Shop and Diner
Cuisines: Breakfast & Brunch, Diner
Average price: Inexpensive
Area: International District
Address: 5801 Central Ave SE
Albuquerque, NM 87123
Phone: (505) 232-9658

#195
Hartford Square
Cuisines: American, Salad
Average price: Modest
Area: Downtown
Address: 300 Broadway Blvd NE
Albuquerque, NM 87102
Phone: (505) 265-4933

#196
Altitude Sports Grill
Cuisines: American, Sports Bar
Average price: Modest
Area: Midtown/University
Address: 2500 Carlisle Blvd NE
Albuquerque, NM 87110
Phone: (505) 855-6085

#197
Gold Street Caffe
Cuisines: Cafe, Sandwiches
Average price: Modest
Area: Downtown
Address: 218 Gold Ave SW
Albuquerque, NM 87102
Phone: (505) 765-1633

#198
Chama River Brewing Company
Cuisines: Brewery, American
Average price: Modest
Area: Business Parkway/Academy Acres
Address: 4939 Pan American W Fwy
Albuquerque, NM 87109
Phone: (505) 342-1800

#199
Yummi House
Cuisines: Chinese
Average price: Inexpensive
Area: Eastside
Address: 1404 Eubank Blvd NE
Albuquerque, NM 87112
Phone: (505) 271-8700

#200
Lucky Boy Restaurant
Cuisines: American
Average price: Inexpensive
Area: Midtown/University
Address: 3521 Constitution Ave NE
Albuquerque, NM 87106
Phone: (505) 268-2785

#201
Viet Deli
Cuisines: Vietnamese,
Asian Fusion, Vegetarian
Average price: Inexpensive
Area: Eastside
Address: 1301 Eubank NE
Albuquerque, NM 87112
Phone: (505) 990-0480

#202
An Hy Quan Vegetarian Restaurant
Cuisines: Vietnamese, Vegetarian, Vegan
Average price: Modest
Area: Eastside
Address: 1405 Juan Tabo Blvd NE
Albuquerque, NM 87112
Phone: (505) 332-8565

#203
Talking Drums Restaurant
Cuisines: African
Average price: Modest
Area: Midtown/University
Address: 1606 Central Ave SE
Albuquerque, NM 87106
Phone: (505) 792-3221

#204
Papaburgers
Cuisines: Burgers
Average price: Inexpensive
Area: North Valley/Los Ranchos
Address: 6601 4th St NW
Albuquerque, NM 87107
Phone: (505) 345-0255

#205
St. James Tearoom
Cuisines: Tea Room, British,
Venue & Event Space
Average price: Expensive
Area: Business Parkway/Academy Acres
Address: 320 Osuna NE
Albuquerque, NM 87107
Phone: (505) 242-3752

#206
Pacific Paradise
Cuisines: Sushi Bar
Average price: Modest
Area: Business Parkway/Academy Acres
Address: 3000 San Pedro Dr NE
Albuquerque, NM 87110
Phone: (505) 881-0999

#207
Hot Pink Thai Cuisine
Cuisines: Thai
Average price: Modest
Area: Uptown
Address: 2626 San Pedro Blvd NE
Albuquerque, NM 87110
Phone: (505) 872-2296

#208
Adoughbe Pizza
Cuisines: Food Truck, Pizza
Average price: Modest
Area: Barelas/South Valley
Address: 318 Isleta Blvd SW
Albuquerque, NM 87105
Phone: (505) 333-9006

#209
Hibachi One
Cuisines: Sushi Bar, Japanese, Steakhouse
Average price: Modest
Area: North Valley/Los Ranchos
Address: 3230 Coors Blvd. NW
Albuquerque, NM 87120
Phone: (505) 839-0808

#210
Loyola's Family Restaurant
Cuisines: Mexican, Diner, Breakfast & Brunch
Average price: Inexpensive
Area: Midtown/University
Address: 4500 Central Ave SE
Albuquerque, NM 87108
Phone: (505) 268-6478

#211
Marley's Texas BBQ
Cuisines: Barbeque
Average price: Modest
Area: Business Parkway/Academy Acres
Address: 7520 4th St NW
Albuquerque, NM 87107
Phone: (505) 585-3661

#212
Cafe 66
Cuisines: Mexican
Average price: Inexpensive
Area: Barelas/South Valley
Address: 9200 Central Ave SW
Albuquerque, NM 87121
Phone: (505) 833-3599

#213
St Clair Winery & Bistro
Cuisines: Winery, Wine Bar, French
Average price: Modest
Area: Old Town
Address: 901 Rio Grande Blvd NW
Albuquerque, NM 87104
Phone: (505) 243-9916

#214
El Charrito Mexican Restaurant
Cuisines: Mexican
Average price: Modest
Area: Westside
Address: 4703 Central Ave NW
Albuquerque, NM 87105
Phone: (505) 836-2464

#215
Middle Eastern Food & Kabobs
Cuisines: Halal, Middle Eastern, Sandwiches
Average price: Inexpensive
Area: Midtown/University
Address: 4801 Central Ave NE
Albuquerque, NM 87108
Phone: (505) 255-5151

#216
Federico's Mexican Food
Cuisines: Mexican
Average price: Inexpensive
Area: Eastside
Address: 1109 Juan Tabo Blvd
Albuquerque, NM 87112
Phone: (505) 271-6499

#217
Ruth's Chris Steak House
Cuisines: Steakhouse
Average price: Exclusive
Area: Uptown
Address: 6640 Indian School Rd NE
Albuquerque, NM 87110
Phone: (505) 884-3350

#218
The Cheesecake Factory
Cuisines: Desserts, American
Average price: Modest
Area: Uptown
Address: 6600 Menaul Blvd NE
Albuquerque, NM 87110
Phone: (505) 883-2539

#219
Ortega's Mexican Restaurant
Cuisines: Mexican
Average price: Inexpensive
Area: Business Parkway/Academy Acres
Address: 3617 Wyoming Blvd NE
Albuquerque, NM 87111
Phone: (505) 298-0223

#220
The Daily Grind
Cuisines: Coffee & Tea, American,
Breakfast & Brunch
Average price: Modest
Area: Midtown/University
Address: 4360 Cutler Ave
Albuquerque, NM 87110
Phone: (505) 883-8310

#221
Q Burger
Cuisines: Burgers
Average price: Modest
Area: Downtown
Address: 301 Central NW
Albuquerque, NM 87102
Phone: (505) 224-2747

#222
Grassburger
Cuisines: American, Burgers, Vegan
Average price: Modest
Area: Eastside
Address: 11225 Montgomery Blvd
Albuquerque, NM 87111
Phone: (505) 200-0571

#223
Baggin's Gourmet Sandwiches
Cuisines: Sandwiches, Desserts, Deli
Average price: Inexpensive
Area: Uptown, International District
Address: 5900 Lomas Blvd NE
Albuquerque, NM 87110
Phone: (505) 262-1451

#224
Straight Up Pizza
Cuisines: Pizza
Average price: Modest
Area: Eastside
Address: 2801 Eubank Blvd
Albuquerque, NM 87112
Phone: (505) 796-9343

#225
La Quiche Parisienne Bistro
Cuisines: Cafe, French, Breakfast & Brunch
Average price: Modest
Area: Eastside
Address: 5850 Eubank Blvd NE, Ste 17
Albuquerque, NM 87111
Phone: (505) 242-2808

#226
Gecko's Bar & Tapas
Cuisines: American, Gastropub, Tapas Bar
Average price: Modest
Area: Nob Hill
Address: 3500 Central Ave SE
Albuquerque, NM 87106
Phone: (505) 262-1848

#227
Thai Cuisine II
Cuisines: Thai, Vegan
Average price: Modest
Area: Nob Hill
Address: 4201 Central Ave NE
Albuquerque, NM 87108
Phone: (505) 232-3200

#228
Bull Chicks
Cuisines: Burgers, Salad, Chicken Wings
Average price: Inexpensive
Area: Eastside
Address: 4400 Wyoming Blvd NE
Albuquerque, NM 87111
Phone: (505) 639-5430

#229
Nob Hill Bar & Grill
Cuisines: American
Average price: Modest
Area: Nob Hill
Address: 3128 Central Ave SE
Albuquerque, NM 87106
Phone: (505) 266-4455

#230
Alien Brew Pub
Cuisines: Pub, Burgers, Beer Bar
Average price: Modest
Area: Uptown
Address: 6601 Uptown Blvd NE
Albuquerque, NM 87110
Phone: (505) 884-1116

#231
Sadie's on Academy
Cuisines: Mexican
Average price: Modest
Area: Business Parkway/Academy Acres
Address: 5400 Academy Rd NE
Albuquerque, NM 87109
Phone: (505) 821-3388

#232
Los Cuates
Cuisines: Mexican
Average price: Modest
Area: Midtown/University
Address: 4901 Lomas Blvd NE
Albuquerque, NM 87110
Phone: (505) 255-5079

#233
Kolache Factory
Cuisines: Bakery, Breakfast & Brunch
Average price: Inexpensive
Area: Business Parkway/Academy Acres
Address: 8001 Wyoming Blvd NE
Albuquerque, NM 87113
Phone: (505) 856-3430

#234
Mimmo's Ristorante & Pizzeria
Cuisines: Italian, Pizza
Average price: Modest
Area: Westside
Address: 3301 Coors Blvd NW
Albuquerque, NM 87120
Phone: (505) 831-4191

#235
Jinja Bar & Bistro
Cuisines: American, Asian Fusion, Sushi Bar
Average price: Modest
Area: Westside
Address: 5400 Sevilla Ave NW
Albuquerque, NM 87120
Phone: (505) 792-8776

#236
The Original Garcia's Kitchen
Cuisines: Mexican
Average price: Inexpensive
Area: Downtown
Address: 1113 4th St NW
Albuquerque, NM 87102
Phone: (505) 247-9149

#237
Saggios
Cuisines: Pizza, Italian, Sports Bar
Average price: Inexpensive
Area: Midtown/University
Address: 107 Cornell Dr SE
Albuquerque, NM 87106
Phone: (505) 255-5454

#238
Urban Hotdog Company
Cuisines: Hot Dogs
Average price: Inexpensive
Area: North Valley/Los Ranchos
Address: 10250 Cottonwood Park Dr NW
Albuquerque, NM 87114
Phone: (505) 898-5671

#239
Delicias Cafe
Cuisines: Mexican, Cafe
Average price: Modest
Area: Business Parkway/Academy Acres
Address: 6001 San Mateo NE
Albuquerque, NM 87109
Phone: (505) 830-6561

#240
Bonefish Grill
Cuisines: Seafood
Average price: Modest
Area: Uptown
Address: 6600 Menaul Blvd. NE
Albuquerque, NM 87110
Phone: (505) 881-2449

#241
Jasmine Thai & Sushi House
Cuisines: Thai
Average price: Modest
Area: Business Parkway/Academy Acres
Address: 4320 The 25 Way
Albuquerque, NM 87109
Phone: (505) 345-0960

#242
AmerAsia-Sumosushi
Cuisines: Dim Sum, Sushi Bar
Average price: Modest
Area: Downtown
Address: 800 3rd St NW
Albuquerque, NM 87102
Phone: (505) 246-1615

#243
Pop-Pop's Italian Ice
Cuisines: Ice Cream, Italian, Fast Food
Average price: Inexpensive
Area: Eastside
Address: 9880 Montgomery Blvd NE
Albuquerque, NM 87111
Phone: (505) 293-8446

#244
Flying Star Cafe
Cuisines: American, Bakery,
Breakfast & Brunch
Average price: Modest
Area: North Valley/Los Ranchos
Address: 4026 Rio Grande NW
Albuquerque, NM 87107
Phone: (505) 344-6714

#245
Swiss Alps Bakery
Cuisines: Specialty Food, Bakery, Cafe
Average price: Inexpensive
Area: Business Parkway/Academy Acres
Address: 3000 San Pedro NE
Albuquerque, NM 87110
Phone: (505) 881-3063

#246
Brickyard Pizza
Cuisines: Pizza
Average price: Inexpensive
Area: Midtown/University
Address: 2216 Central Ave SE
Albuquerque, NM 87106
Phone: (505) 262-2216

#247
Perico's Albuquerque
Cuisines: Mexican
Average price: Inexpensive
Area: North Valley/Los Ranchos
Address: 2810 Coors Blvd NW
Albuquerque, NM 87120
Phone: (505) 839-4762

#248
Thai Tip
Cuisines: Thai
Average price: Modest
Area: Eastside
Address: 1512 Wyoming Blvd NE
Albuquerque, NM 87112
Phone: (505) 323-7447

#249
La Crêpe Michel
Cuisines: French
Average price: Modest
Area: Old Town
Address: 400 San Felipe St NW
Albuquerque, NM 87104
Phone: (505) 242-1251

#250
Garcia's Kitchen-the Original
Cuisines: Mexican
Average price: Inexpensive
Area: Old Town
Address: 1736 Central Ave SW
Albuquerque, NM 87104
Phone: (505) 242-1199

#251
Cocina Azul
Cuisines: Mexican
Average price: Modest
Area: Business Parkway/Academy Acres
Address: 4243 Montgomery Blvd NE
Albuquerque, NM 87109
Phone: (505) 831-2600

#252
**Pupuseria Y Restaurante
Salvadoreno**
Cuisines: Latin American
Average price: Inexpensive
Area: Barelas/South Valley
Address: 1701 Bridge Blvd SW
Albuquerque, NM 87105
Phone: (505) 243-8194

#253
Old Town Pizza Parlor
Cuisines: Pizza, Italian, Caterer
Average price: Modest
Area: Old Town
Address: 108 Rio Grande Blvd NW
Albuquerque, NM 87104
Phone: (505) 999-1949

#254
MAS - Tapas Y Vino
Cuisines: Tapas/Small Plates,
Breakfast & Brunch
Average price: Modest
Area: Downtown
Address: 125 2nd St NW
Albuquerque, NM 87102
Phone: (505) 923-9080

#255
Chicharroneria Orozco
Cuisines: Mexican
Average price: Inexpensive
Area: International District
Address: 1218 San Pedro SE
Albuquerque, NM 87105
Phone: (505) 480-4751

#256
66 Diner
Cuisines: Diner, Burgers, American
Average price: Modest
Area: Midtown/University
Address: 1405 Central Ave NE
Albuquerque, NM 87106
Phone: (505) 247-1421

#257
El Pinto
Cuisines: Mexican, Salad, Gluten-Free
Average price: Modest
Area: Business Parkway/Academy Acres
Address: 10500 4th St NW
Albuquerque, NM 87114
Phone: (505) 898-1771

#258
The Lunch Box Food Truck
Cuisines: Food Truck, Sandwiches
Average price: Modest
Area: North Valley/Los Ranchos
Address: 9000 Coors Blvd
Albuquerque, NM 87120
Phone: (505) 350-2827

#259
Fai Wong Chinese Restaurant
Cuisines: Shanghainese
Average price: Inexpensive
Area: North Valley/Los Ranchos
Address: 6200 Coors Blvd NW
Albuquerque, NM 87120
Phone: (505) 243-0290

#260
Monte Vista Fire Station
Cuisines: American, Pub
Average price: Modest
Area: Nob Hill
Address: 3201 Central Ave Ne
Albuquerque, NM 87106
Phone: (505) 255-2424

#261
Sakura Sushi and Grill
Cuisines: Japanese, Korean, Sushi Bar
Average price: Modest
Area: North Valley/Los Ranchos
Address: 6241 Riverside Plaza Ln
Albuquerque, NM 87120
Phone: (505) 890-2838

#262
Hannah and Nate's
Cuisines: Breakfast & Brunch
Average price: Inexpensive
Area: North Valley/Los Ranchos
Address: 6251 Riverside Plz Ln NW
Albuquerque, NM 87120
Phone: (505) 922-1155

#263
Asian Grill
Cuisines: Asian Fusion
Average price: Inexpensive
Area: International District
Address: 5303 Gibson Blvd SE
Albuquerque, NM 87108
Phone: (505) 265-4702

#264
Barelas Coffee House
Cuisines: Coffee & Tea, Mexican
Average price: Inexpensive
Area: Barelas/South Valley
Address: 1502 4th St SW
Albuquerque, NM 87102
Phone: (505) 843-7577

#265
Backstreet Grill
Cuisines: Mexican, Bar, American
Average price: Modest
Area: Old Town
Address: 1919 Old Town Rd NW
Albuquerque, NM 87104
Phone: (505) 842-5434

#266
Tenampa
Cuisines: Mexican
Average price: Inexpensive
Area: Westside
Address: 101 98th St NW
Albuquerque, NM 87121
Phone: (505) 352-5500

#267
BJ's Restaurant & Brewhouse
Cuisines: Brewery, American, Pizza
Average price: Modest
Area: Uptown
Address: 2100 Louisiana Blvd. NE
Albuquerque, NM 87110
Phone: (505) 872-8600

#268
Milly's Sandwich Shop
Cuisines: Salad, Sandwiches
Average price: Inexpensive
Area: Business Parkway/Academy Acres
Address: 7308 Jefferson St NE
Albuquerque, NM 87109
Phone: (505) 345-9200

#269
Japanese Kitchen Sushi Bar
Cuisines: Japanese, Sushi Bar
Average price: Modest
Area: Uptown
Address: 6511 Americas Pkwy NE
Albuquerque, NM 87110
Phone: (505) 872-1166

#270
Sushi Xuan
Cuisines: Sushi Bar, Japanese, Asian Fusion
Average price: Modest
Area: Westside
Address: 8201 Golf Course Rd NW
Albuquerque, NM 87120
Phone: (505) 898-6666

#271
Which Wich
Cuisines: Sandwiches
Average price: Inexpensive
Area: Midtown/University
Address: 2300 Central Ave SE
Albuquerque, NM 87106
Phone: (505) 254-4749

#272
M'tucci's Cocina Grill
Cuisines: Latin American
Average price: Modest
Area: Barelas/South Valley
Address: 1701 4th St SW
Albuquerque, NM 87102
Phone: (505) 242-3564

#273
Gatos Y Galletas Cat Cafe
Cuisines: Coffee & Tea, Juice Bar,
Vegetarian
Average price: Modest
Area: Downtown
Address: 414 Central Ave SE
Albuquerque, NM 87102
Phone: (505) 243-9955

#274
Taj Mahal Cuisine Of India
Cuisines: Vegetarian, Indian, Pakistani
Average price: Modest
Area: Midtown/University
Address: 1430 Carlisle Blvd NE
Albuquerque, NM 87110
Phone: (505) 255-1994

#275
Mr Powdrell's Barbeque
Cuisines: Barbeque
Average price: Modest
Area: Eastside
Address: 11301 Central Ave NE
Albuquerque, NM 87123
Phone: (505) 298-6766

#276
Duggan's Coffee
Cuisines: Breakfast & Brunch
Average price: Inexpensive
Area: Midtown/University
Address: 2227 Lead Ave SE
Albuquerque, NM 87106
Phone: (505) 312-7257

#277
ChopstiX Chinese Cuisine
Cuisines: Chinese
Average price: Modest
Area: Uptown
Address: 6001-L Lomas Blvd NE
Albuquerque, NM 87108
Phone: (505) 268-8777

#278
Fiesta's
Cuisines: Mexican
Average price: Modest
Area: Business Parkway/Academy Acres
Address: 4400 Carlisle Blvd NE
Albuquerque, NM 87107
Phone: (505) 881-0478

#279
El Bruno's
Cuisines: Mexican
Average price: Modest
Area: Business Parkway/Academy Acres
Address: 8806 4th St NW
Albuquerque, NM 87114
Phone: (505) 897-0444

#280
Scalo Northern Italian Grill
Cuisines: Italian
Average price: Modest
Area: Nob Hill
Address: 3500 Central Ave SE
Albuquerque, NM 87106
Phone: (505) 255-8781

#281
Western View Diner & Steakhouse
Cuisines: American, Diner
Average price: Modest
Area: Westside
Address: 6411 Central Ave NW
Albuquerque, NM 87105
Phone: (505) 836-2200

#282
Jersey Mike's Subs
Cuisines: Deli, Fast Food, Sandwiches
Average price: Inexpensive
Area: Eastside
Address: 9500 Montgomery Blvd N.E.
Albuquerque, NM 87111
Phone: (505) 323-0077

#283
Monroe's Restaurant
Cuisines: Mexican
Average price: Modest
Area: Business Parkway/Academy Acres
Address: 6051 Osuna Rd NE
Albuquerque, NM 87109
Phone: (505) 881-4224

#284
Slice Parlor
Cuisines: Pizza, Salad
Average price: Inexpensive
Area: Eastside
Address: 9904 Montgomery Blvd NE
Albuquerque, NM 87111
Phone: (505) 232-2808

#285
Little Anita's
Cuisines: Mexican, Salad, Sandwiches
Average price: Inexpensive
Area: Airport/Base
Address: 3041 University Blvd SE
Albuquerque, NM 87106
Phone: (505) 924-3029

#286
Juanita's Comida Mexicana
Cuisines: Mexican
Average price: Inexpensive
Area: Barelas/South Valley
Address: 910 4th St SW
Albuquerque, NM 87102
Phone: (505) 843-9669

#287
Thai Kitchen
Cuisines: Thai
Average price: Modest
Area: North Valley/Los Ranchos
Address: 10701 Corrales Rd NW
Albuquerque, NM 87114
Phone: (505) 890-0059

#288
Salathai
Cuisines: Thai
Average price: Inexpensive
Area: Nob Hill
Address: 3619 Copper Ave NE
Albuquerque, NM 87108
Phone: (505) 265-9330

#289
Bob's Burgers
Cuisines: American
Average price: Inexpensive
Area: Barelas/South Valley
Address: 4506 Central Ave SW
Albuquerque, NM 87105
Phone: (505) 831-2111

#290
Fans Of Film Cafe & Roaster
Cuisines: Coffee & Tea, Cafe
Average price: Inexpensive
Area: Airport/Base
Address: 504 Yale Blvd SE
Albuquerque, NM 87106
Phone: (505) 200-0243

#291
Flying Star Cafe
Cuisines: Bakery, American,
Breakfast & Brunch
Average price: Modest
Area: Nob Hill
Address: 3416 Central Ave SE
Albuquerque, NM 87106
Phone: (505) 255-6633

#292
Thai House
Cuisines: Thai
Average price: Inexpensive
Area: Midtown/University
Address: 106 Buena Vista Dr SE
Albuquerque, NM 87106
Phone: (505) 247-9205

#293
Olive Branch Bistro
Cuisines: Mediterranean, American, Greek
Average price: Modest
Area: Business Parkway/Academy Acres
Address: 6910 Montgomery Blvd NE
Albuquerque, NM 87110
Phone: (505) 881-2291

#294
Mr. Powdrell's Barbeque House
Cuisines: Barbeque
Average price: Modest
Area: North Valley/Los Ranchos
Address: 5209 4th St NW
Albuquerque, NM 87107
Phone: (505) 345-8086

#295
Garduno's
Cuisines: Mexican, Salad, Burgers
Average price: Modest
Area: Uptown
Address: 2100 Louisiana Blvd NE
Albuquerque, NM 87110
Phone: (505) 880-0055

#296
Vintage 423
Cuisines: American, Steakhouse, American
Average price: Expensive
Area: Eastside
Address: 8000 Paseo Del Norte Blvd
Albuquerque, NM 87109
Phone: (505) 821-1918

#297
Ironwood Kitchen
Cuisines: Comfort Food, American
Average price: Inexpensive
Area: Westside
Address: 5740 Night Whisper Rd NW
Albuquerque, NM 87114
Phone: (505) 890-4488

#298
Times Square Deli Mart
Cuisines: Convenience Store, Deli,
Sandwiches
Average price: Inexpensive
Area: Midtown/University
Address: 2132 Central Ave SE
Albuquerque, NM 87106
Phone: (505) 242-0809

#299
Thai Vegan
Cuisines: Vegan, Thai
Average price: Modest
Area: Business Parkway/Academy Acres
Address: 5505 Osuna Rd NE
Albuquerque, NM 87109
Phone: (505) 884-4610

#300
Texas Roadhouse
Cuisines: Steakhouse, Barbeque, American
Average price: Modest
Area: Business Parkway/Academy Acres
Address: 5900 Pan American Frontage Rd N
Albuquerque, NM 87109
Phone: (505) 856-2226

#301
Rex's Hamburgers
Cuisines: Burgers
Average price: Inexpensive
Area: Business Parkway/Academy Acres
Address: 5555 Montgomery Blvd
Albuquerque, NM 87109
Phone: (505) 837-2827

#302
Dakine Hawaiian Ice & Purified Water
Cuisines: Hawaiian, Shaved Ice
Average price: Inexpensive
Area: Business Parkway/Academy Acres
Address: 4007 Carlisle Blvd NE
Albuquerque, NM 87107
Phone: (505) 821-8402

#303
Deep Space Coffee
Cuisines: Coffee & Tea, Cafe
Average price: Inexpensive
Area: Downtown
Address: 504 Central Ave SW
Albuquerque, NM 87102
Phone: (505) 322-2812

#304
Taaj Palace
Cuisines: Indian
Average price: Modest
Area: Eastside
Address: 1435 Eubank Blvd NE
Albuquerque, NM 87112
Phone: (505) 296-0109

#305
Weck's
Cuisines: Breakfast & Brunch
Average price: Inexpensive
Area: Business Parkway/Academy Acres
Address: 4500 Osuna Rd NE
Albuquerque, NM 87109
Phone: (505) 344-1472

#306
Whole Hog Cafe
Cuisines: Barbeque
Average price: Modest
Area: Eastside
Address: 9880 Montgomery Blvd NE
Albuquerque, NM 87111
Phone: (505) 323-1688

#307
Nick & Jimmy's Bar and Grill
Cuisines: American, Steakhouse, Greek
Average price: Modest
Area: Business Parkway/Academy Acres
Address: 5021 Pan American W Fwy NE
Albuquerque, NM 87109
Phone: (505) 344-9169

#308
Amore Neapolitan Pizzeria
Cuisines: Pizza
Average price: Modest
Area: Old Town
Address: 1700 Central Ave SW
Albuquerque, NM 87104
Phone: (505) 312-8784

#309
A-1 Oriental Market
Cuisines: Korean, International Grocery
Average price: Modest
Area: Business Parkway/Academy Acres
Address: 6207 Montgomery Blvd NE
Albuquerque, NM 87109
Phone: (505) 275-9021

#310
Richard's Mexican Restaurant
Cuisines: Mexican
Average price: Inexpensive
Area: Midtown/University
Address: 3301 Menaul Blvd NE
Albuquerque, NM 87107
Phone: (505) 881-1039

#311
Cinnamon Sugar and Spice Cafe
Cuisines: Breakfast & Brunch,
Coffee & Tea, Internet Cafe
Average price: Modest
Area: Eastside
Address: 5809 Juan Tabo NE
Albuquerque, NM 87111
Phone: (505) 492-2119

#312
Ruben's Grill
Cuisines: Mexican
Average price: Inexpensive
Area: Eastside
Address: 9708 Candelaria Rd NE
Albuquerque, NM 87112
Phone: (505) 294-1900

#313
Duran's Station
Cuisines: Mexican
Average price: Modest
Area: Midtown/University
Address: 4201 Menaul Blvd NE
Albuquerque, NM 87110
Phone: (505) 830-0007

#314
Bricklight DIVE
Cuisines: Pizza, Gastropub, Italian
Average price: Inexpensive
Area: Midtown/University
Address: 115 Harvard SE C9
Albuquerque, NM 87106
Phone: (505) 232-7000

#315
Elephant Bar Restaurant
Cuisines: American, Bar, Asian Fusion
Average price: Modest
Area: Uptown
Address: 2240 Louisiana Blvd
Albuquerque, NM 87110
Phone: (505) 884-2355

#316
Sushi Hana
Cuisines: Sushi Bar, Japanese
Average price: Modest
Area: Downtown
Address: 521 Central Ave Nw
Albuquerque, NM 87102
Phone: (505) 842-8700

#317
Thai Vegan
Cuisines: Thai, Vegan
Average price: Modest
Area: Nob Hill
Address: 3804 Central Ave SE
Albuquerque, NM 87108
Phone: (505) 200-2290

#318
Naka Sushi
Cuisines: Sushi Bar, Japanese
Average price: Modest
Area: Eastside
Address: 1035 Juan Tabo Blvd NE
Albuquerque, NM 87112
Phone: (505) 200-9152

#319
Sushiya
Cuisines: Asian Fusion, Sushi Bar, Japanese
Average price: Modest
Area: Eastside
Address: 2906 Juan Tabo Blvd NE
Albuquerque, NM 87112
Phone: (505) 275-4777

#320
Paisano's
Cuisines: Italian, Gluten-Free
Average price: Modest
Area: Eastside
Address: 1935 Eubank Blvd NE
Albuquerque, NM 87112
Phone: (505) 298-7541

#321
Murphy's Mule Barn
Cuisines: Breakfast & Brunch, Diner,
American
Average price: Inexpensive
Area: Business Parkway/Academy Acres
Address: 9700 2nd St NW
Albuquerque, NM 87114
Phone: (505) 898-7660

#322
Papa Felipe's Mexican Restaurant
Cuisines: Mexican
Average price: Modest
Area: Eastside
Address: 9800 Menaul Blvd NE
Albuquerque, NM 87112
Phone: (505) 292-8877

#323
Zorba's Fine Greek Cuisine
Cuisines: Greek, Mediterranean
Average price: Modest
Area: Eastside
Address: 11225 Montgomery Blvd NE
Albuquerque, NM 87111
Phone: (505) 323-2695

#324
Saigon Restaurant
Cuisines: Vietnamese
Average price: Inexpensive
Area: Business Parkway/Academy Acres
Address: 6001 San Mateo Blvd NE
Albuquerque, NM 87109
Phone: (505) 884-0706

#325
Draft Station ABQ
Cuisines: Pub, Beer, American
Average price: Inexpensive
Area: Old Town
Address: 1726 Central Ave Sw
Albuquerque, NM 87104
Phone: (505) 247-0193

#326
A Taste of the Carribean
Cuisines: Caribbean
Average price: Modest
Area: Midtown/University
Address: 2720 Central Ave SE
Albuquerque, NM 87106
Phone: (505) 503-8428

#327
5 Star Burgers
Cuisines: American, Burgers
Average price: Modest
Area: Business Parkway/Academy Acres
Address: 5901 Wyoming Blvd NE
Albuquerque, NM 87109
Phone: (505) 821-1909

#328
Christy Mae's Restaurant
Cuisines: Sandwiches
Average price: Modest
Area: Uptown
Address: 1400 San Pedro Dr NE
Albuquerque, NM 87110
Phone: (505) 255-4740

#329
Golden Pride Bbq Chicken & Ribs
Cuisines: Barbeque
Average price: Inexpensive
Area: Westside
Address: 5231 Central Ave NW
Albuquerque, NM 87105
Phone: (505) 836-1544

#330
Luigi's Restaurant & Pizzeria
Cuisines: Pizza
Average price: Modest
Area: North Valley/Los Ranchos
Address: 6225 4th St Nw
Albuquerque, NM 87107
Phone: (505) 343-0466

#331
Four Joys Chinese Restaurant
Cuisines: Chinese
Average price: Inexpensive
Area: Business Parkway/Academy Acres,
North Valley/Los Ranchos
Address: 6122 4th St NW
Albuquerque, NM 87107
Phone: (505) 345-5975

#332
**Freddy's Frozen Custard
& Steakburgers**
Cuisines: Burgers, Ice Cream
Average price: Inexpensive
Area: Business Parkway/Academy Acres
Address: 6240 Paseo Del Norte NE
Albuquerque, NM 87113
Phone: (505) 796-9020

#333
Albuquerque City Limits Restaurant
Cuisines: American
Average price: Inexpensive
Area: Barelas/South Valley
Address: 3231 Coors Blvd SW
Albuquerque, NM 87121
Phone: (505) 873-8959

#334
Christee's Spuds Burgers & More
Cuisines: American, Burgers
Average price: Inexpensive
Area: Eastside
Address: 1945 Juan Tabo Blvd NE
Albuquerque, NM 87112
Phone: (505) 275-8334

#335
Rose Garden
Cuisines: Fast Food, Chinese
Average price: Inexpensive
Area: Westside
Address: 6541 Paradise Blvd NW
Albuquerque, NM 87114
Phone: (505) 897-8880

#336
Relish Gourmet Sandwiches
Cuisines: Sandwiches, Salad, Vegetarian
Average price: Modest
Area: Uptown
Address: 8019 Menaul Blvd NE
Albuquerque, NM 87110
Phone: (505) 299-0001

#337
Slate at the Museum
Cuisines: Cafe, Museums
Average price: Modest
Area: Old Town
Address: 2000 Mountain Rd NW
Albuquerque, NM 87104
Phone: (505) 243-2220

#338
Friends Coffee & Sandwich
Cuisines: Bagels, Breakfast & Brunch
Average price: Inexpensive
Area: Downtown
Address: 200 3rd St NW
Albuquerque, NM 87102
Phone: (505) 243-4801

#339
Rustic A Divine Food Truck
Cuisines: American, Food Truck
Average price: Modest
Area: Downtown
Address: 111 Marble Ave NW
Albuquerque, NM 87102
Phone: (505) 944-5849

#340
Sandia Chile Grill
Cuisines: Mexican, Brewery
Average price: Inexpensive
Area: Eastside
Address: 7120 Wyoming Blvd NE
Albuquerque, NM 87109
Phone: (505) 798-1970

#341
El Patron Restaurant & Cantina
Cuisines: Mexican
Average price: Modest
Area: Eastside
Address: 10551 Montgomery Blvd NE
Albuquerque, NM 87111
Phone: (505) 275-0223

#342
Kathy's
Cuisines: Mexican
Average price: Inexpensive
Area: Barelas/South Valley
Address: 823 Isleta Blvd SW
Albuquerque, NM 87105
Phone: (505) 873-3472

#343
Kyana's Kitchen
Cuisines: Vietnamese, Soup
Average price: Inexpensive
Area: Downtown
Address: 315 Gold Ave SW
Albuquerque, NM 87102
Phone: (505) 503-8899

#344
Copper Canyon Cafe
Cuisines: Mexican, American
Average price: Inexpensive
Area: International District
Address: 5455 Gibson Blvd SE
Albuquerque, NM 87108
Phone: (505) 266-6318

#345
Slice Parlor
Cuisines: Pizza
Average price: Inexpensive
Area: Nob Hill
Address: 3410 Central Ave SE
Albuquerque, NM 87106
Phone: (505) 232-2808

#346
Twisters Burgers & Burritos
Cuisines: Breakfast & Brunch,
Burgers, Mexican
Average price: Inexpensive
Area: Business Parkway/Academy Acres
Address: 7600 Jefferson St NE
Albuquerque, NM 87109
Phone: (505) 821-6184

#347
Quesadilla Grille
Cuisines: Mexican, Bar, Diner
Average price: Modest
Area: Old Town
Address: 328 San Felipe St NW
Albuquerque, NM 87104
Phone: (505) 242-2921

#348
Claim Jumper
Cuisines: Steakhouse, American, Bar
Average price: Modest
Area: Business Parkway/Academy Acres
Address: 5001 Jefferson St NE
Albuquerque, NM 87109
Phone: (505) 872-2155

#349
Twin Peaks
Cuisines: American, Sports Bar, American
Average price: Modest
Area: Business Parkway/Academy Acres
Address: 4441 The 25 Way NE
Albuquerque, NM 87109
Phone: (505) 343-8500

#350
Weck's
Cuisines: Breakfast & Brunch
Average price: Inexpensive
Area: North Valley/Los Ranchos
Address: 6311 Riverside Plaza Ln
Albuquerque, NM 87120
Phone: (505) 352-6209

#351
Pita Pit
Cuisines: Greek, Mediterranean, Sandwiches
Average price: Inexpensive
Area: Midtown/University
Address: 2106 Central Ave SE
Albuquerque, NM 87106
Phone: (505) 242-7482

#352
The Yeller Sub
Cuisines: Sandwiches
Average price: Inexpensive
Area: Business Parkway/Academy Acres
Address: 7200 Montgomery Blvd NE
Albuquerque, NM 87109
Phone: (505) 888-9784

#353
Korean BBQ House
Cuisines: Korean
Average price: Modest
Area: Nob Hill
Address: 3200 Central Ave SE
Albuquerque, NM 87106
Phone: (505) 338-2424

#354
Little Anita's
Cuisines: Mexican
Average price: Modest
Area: Old Town
Address: 2105 Mountain Rd NW
Albuquerque, NM 87104
Phone: (505) 242-3102

#355
Le Peep Restaurant
Cuisines: Breakfast & Brunch
Average price: Modest
Area: Uptown
Address: 2125 Louisiana Blvd NE
Albuquerque, NM 87110
Phone: (505) 881-7272

#356
Marcello's Chophouse
Cuisines: Steakhouse, American, Wine Bar
Average price: Expensive
Area: Uptown
Address: 2201 Q St NE
Albuquerque, NM 87110
Phone: (505) 837-2467

#357
Bubba's 33
Cuisines: Burgers, Pizza, American
Average price: Modest
Area: Business Parkway/Academy Acres
Address: 4861 Pan American Freeway
Albuquerque, NM 87109
Phone: (505) 344-7427

#358
Taco Cabana
Cuisines: Mexican
Average price: Inexpensive
Area: Business Parkway/Academy Acres
Address: 8330 Montgomery Blvd
Albuquerque, NM 87111
Phone: (505) 275-2600

#359
Ricas Gorditas Vale
Cuisines: Food Truck, Mexican
Average price: Inexpensive
Area: Barelas/South Valley
Address: 3311 Coors Blvd SW
Albuquerque, NM 87121
Phone: (505) 319-3063

#360
Jimmy John's
Cuisines: Sandwiches
Average price: Inexpensive
Area: Midtown/University
Address: 2132 Central Ave SE
Albuquerque, NM 87106
Phone: (505) 243-8888

#361
Albuquerque Café
Cuisines: American
Average price: Inexpensive
Area: Business Parkway/Academy Acres
Address: 4374 Alexander Blvd NE
Albuquerque, NM 87107
Phone: (505) 344-6666

#362
LongHorn Steakhouse
Cuisines: Steakhouse, Barbeque, American
Average price: Modest
Area: Uptown
Address: 6600 Menaul Blvd NE
Albuquerque, NM 87110
Phone: (505) 881-5359

#363
Taco Mex
Cuisines: Seafood, Mexican
Average price: Inexpensive
Area: Westside
Address: 640 Coors NW
Albuquerque, NM 87121
Phone: (505) 352-6000

#364
Dion's
Cuisines: Pizza, Sandwiches, Salad
Average price: Inexpensive
Area: Airport/Base
Address: 1600 Towne Center Ln SE
Albuquerque, NM 87106
Phone: (505) 248-1010

#365
Golden Pride Bbq Chicken & Ribs
Cuisines: Barbeque
Average price: Inexpensive
Area: Midtown/University
Address: 1830 Lomas Blvd NE
Albuquerque, NM 87106
Phone: (505) 242-2181

#366
Golden Pride BBQ Chicken & Ribs
Cuisines: Barbeque
Average price: Inexpensive
Area: Eastside
Address: 10101 Central NE
Albuquerque, NM 87123
Phone: (505) 293-3531

#367
Ichiban Japanese Restaurant
Cuisines: Japanese, Sushi Bar, Korean
Average price: Modest
Area: North Valley/Los Ranchos
Address: 10701 Corrales Rd NW
Albuquerque, NM 87111
Phone: (505) 899-0095

#368
Sakura Sushi
Cuisines: Laotian, Sushi Bar, Thai
Average price: Modest
Area: Eastside
Address: 4200 Wyoming Blvd NE
Albuquerque, NM 87111
Phone: (505) 294-9696

#369
Taco Cabana
Cuisines: Mexican
Average price: Inexpensive
Area: Westside
Address: 3301-01 Coors Blvd. NW
Albuquerque, NM 87120
Phone: (505) 836-1650

#370
Itsa Italian Ice
Cuisines: Italian, Ice Cream
Average price: Inexpensive
Area: North Valley/Los Ranchos
Address: 215 Phoenix Ave NW
Albuquerque, NM 87107
Phone: (505) 268-2560

#371
Sara's Pastries & Deli
Cuisines: Sandwiches, Peruvian
Average price: Inexpensive
Area: Business Parkway/Academy Acres
Address: 7600 Jefferson St NE
Albuquerque, NM 87109
Phone: (505) 385-8247

#372
Plum Cafe Asian Grill
Cuisines: Asian Fusion
Average price: Modest
Area: Business Parkway/Academy Acres
Address: 4959 Pan America Fwy NE
Albuquerque, NM 87109
Phone: (505) 433-3448

#373
DG's Deli & Market
Cuisines: Deli, Sandwiches
Average price: Inexpensive
Area: Midtown/University
Address: 1418 Dr Martin Luther King
Jr Ave NE, Albuquerque, NM 87106
Phone: (505) 247-3354

#374
Pelican's Restaurant
Cuisines: Seafood
Average price: Modest
Area: Eastside
Address: 9800 Montgomery Blvd NE
Albuquerque, NM 87111
Phone: (505) 298-7678

#375
Casa de Benavidez
Cuisines: Mexican
Average price: Modest
Area: Business Parkway/Academy Acres
Address: 8032 4th St NW
Albuquerque, NM 87114
Phone: (505) 898-3311

#376
The County Line
Cuisines: Barbeque
Average price: Modest
Area: Eastside
Address: 9600 Tramway Blvd NE
Albuquerque, NM 87122
Phone: (505) 856-7477

#377
Blake's Lota Burger
Cuisines: Burgers
Average price: Inexpensive
Area: Old Town
Address: 777 Rio Grande Blvd NW
Albuquerque, NM 87104
Phone: (505) 243-8343

#378
China Inn Restaurant
Cuisines: Chinese
Average price: Inexpensive
Area: Eastside
Address: 9500 Montgomery Blvd NE
Albuquerque, NM 87111
Phone: (505) 293-4297

#379
Savoy Bar & Grill
Cuisines: American, Wine Bar
Average price: Expensive
Area: Eastside
Address: 10601 Montgomery Blvd NE
Albuquerque, NM 87111
Phone: (505) 294-9463

#380
The Cooperage Restaurant
Cuisines: Steakhouse, Bar
Average price: Modest
Area: International District
Address: 7220 Lomas Blvd NE
Albuquerque, NM 87110
Phone: (505) 255-1657

#381
Teriyaki Chicken Bowl
Cuisines: Japanese
Average price: Inexpensive
Area: Old Town
Address: 2129 Central Ave NW
Albuquerque, NM 87104
Phone: (505) 242-3237

#382
Kai's Chinese Restaurant
Cuisines: Chinese
Average price: Inexpensive
Area: Midtown/University
Address: 138 Harvard Dr SE
Albuquerque, NM 87106
Phone: (505) 266-8388

#383
Il Vicino Wood Oven Pizza
Cuisines: Pizza, Italian
Average price: Modest
Area: North Valley/Los Ranchos
Address: 10701 Corrales Blvd
Albuquerque, NM 87114
Phone: (505) 899-7500

#384
Weck's
Cuisines: Breakfast & Brunch
Average price: Inexpensive
Area: Business Parkway/Academy Acres
Address: 3913 Louisiana Blvd NE
Albuquerque, NM 87110
Phone: (505) 881-0019

#385
Orchid Thai Cuisine
Cuisines: Thai, Asian Fusion
Average price: Modest
Area: Nob Hill
Address: 4300 Central Ave SE
Albuquerque, NM 87108
Phone: (505) 265-4047

#386
Dion's
Cuisines: Pizza, Sandwiches, Salad
Average price: Inexpensive
Area: Westside
Address: 121 Coors Blvd NW
Albuquerque, NM 87121
Phone: (505) 831-3131

#387
Dion's
Cuisines: Pizza, Sandwiches, Salad
Average price: Inexpensive
Area: Midtown/University
Address: 4717 Central Ave NE
Albuquerque, NM 87108
Phone: (505) 265-6919

#388
328 Chinese Cuisine
Cuisines: Chinese
Average price: Inexpensive
Area: Uptown
Address: 5617 Menaul Blvd NE
Albuquerque, NM 87110
Phone: (505) 881-4468

#389
Gold Rush Cupcakes
Cuisines: Desserts, Bakery, Deli
Average price: Inexpensive
Area: Downtown
Address: 20 First Plz Ctr NW
Albuquerque, NM 87102
Phone: (505) 247-4653

#390
Sushi-Hama Japanese Restaurant
Cuisines: Japanese, Sushi Bar
Average price: Modest
Area: Eastside
Address: 2918 Eubank Blvd NE
Albuquerque, NM 87111
Phone: (505) 293-6055

#391
Pho Linh Vietnamese Grill
Cuisines: Vietnamese
Average price: Modest
Area: Eastside
Address: 9100 Central Ave SE
Albuquerque, NM 87123
Phone: (505) 266-3368

#392
Castaneda Restaurant & Catering
Cuisines: Food Truck, Mexican
Average price: Modest
Area: Nob Hill
Address: 114 Tulane Dr SE
Albuquerque, NM 87106
Phone: (505) 315-7939

#393
Whataburger
Cuisines: Burgers, Fast Food, American
Average price: Inexpensive
Area: Midtown/University
Address: 2808 Carlisle NE
Albuquerque, NM 87110
Phone: (505) 888-3868

#394
Olympia Cafe
Cuisines: Greek, Mediterranean
Average price: Inexpensive
Area: Midtown/University
Address: 2210 Central Ave SE
Albuquerque, NM 87106
Phone: (505) 266-5222

#395
P.F. Chang's
Cuisines: Chinese, Gluten-Free
Average price: Modest
Area: Business Parkway/Academy Acres
Address: 4440 The 25 Way NE
Albuquerque, NM 87109
Phone: (505) 344-8282

#396
Gen Kai
Cuisines: Japanese
Average price: Inexpensive
Area: International District
Address: 110 B Louisiana Blvd SE
Albuquerque, NM 87108
Phone: (505) 255-0112

#397
Sushi Freak
Cuisines: Sushi Bar, Japanese, Asian Fusion
Average price: Inexpensive
Area: Uptown
Address: 2200 Louisiana Blvd NE
Albuquerque, NM 87110
Phone: (505) 433-4959

#398
Happy Garden
Cuisines: Chinese
Average price: Inexpensive
Area: Eastside
Address: 13170-D Central
Albuquerque, NM 87123
Phone: (505) 293-8887

#399
Weck's
Cuisines: Breakfast & Brunch
Average price: Inexpensive
Area: Midtown/University
Address: 933 San Mateo Blvd NE
Albuquerque, NM 87108
Phone: (505) 265-9237

#400
Golden Pride Bbq Chicken & Ribs
Cuisines: Barbeque
Average price: Inexpensive
Area: Eastside
Address: 3720 Juan Tabo Blvd NE
Albuquerque, NM 87111
Phone: (505) 294-5767

#401
Breakfast Club
Cuisines: Breakfast & Brunch
Average price: Inexpensive
Area: Westside
Address: 640 Coors Blvd NW
Albuquerque, NM 87121
Phone: (505) 831-5918

#402
El Sarape Mexican Restaurant
Cuisines: Mexican
Average price: Modest
Area: Midtown/University
Address: 4119 Central Ave Ne
Albuquerque, NM 87108
Phone: (505) 266-1907

#403
Rio Grande Brew Pub & Grill
Cuisines: American
Average price: Modest
Area: Airport/Base
Address: 2200 Sunport Blvd SE
Albuquerque, NM 87106
Phone: (505) 842-4292

#404
Texas Land & Cattle
Cuisines: Steakhouse, Seafood, American
Average price: Modest
Area: Business Parkway/Academy Acres
Address: 4949 Pan American Frwy. NE
Albuquerque, NM 87109
Phone: (505) 343-9800

#405
Taco Cabana
Cuisines: Mexican
Average price: Inexpensive
Area: Business Parkway/Academy Acres
Address: 6500 San Mateo NE
Albuquerque, NM 87109
Phone: (505) 821-0203

#406
Dion's
Cuisines: Pizza, Sandwiches, Salad
Average price: Inexpensive
Area: Eastside
Address: 11000 Central Ave SE
Albuquerque, NM 87123
Phone: (505) 296-0771

#407
BJ's Restaurant and Brewhouse
Cuisines: Pizza, American, Brewery
Average price: Modest
Area: Westside
Address: 10000 Coors Blvd
Albuquerque, NM 87114
Phone: (505) 545-6040

#408
Little Anita's
Cuisines: Mexican
Average price: Modest
Area: Midtown/University
Address: 2000 Menaul Blvd NE
Albuquerque, NM 87107
Phone: (505) 837-9459

#409
Dragon House
Cuisines: Chinese
Average price: Modest
Area: North Valley/Los Ranchos
Address: 10200 Corrlaes Rd NW
Albuquerque, NM 87114
Phone: (505) 899-8889

#410
Jinja Bar & Bistro
Cuisines: Asian Fusion, Bar
Average price: Modest
Area: Eastside
Address: 8900 Holly Ave NE
Albuquerque, NM 87122
Phone: (505) 856-1413

#411
Jersey Mike's Subs
Cuisines: Deli, Sandwiches, Fast Food
Average price: Modest
Area: Westside
Address: 2621 Coors Blvd.
Albuquerque, NM 87120
Phone: (505) 833-0030

#412
Ojos Locos Sports Cantina
Cuisines: Mexican, Sports Bar
Average price: Modest
Area: Uptown
Address: 2105 Louisiana Blvd
Albuquerque, NM 87110
Phone: (505) 508-0157

#413
WisePies
Cuisines: Salad, Pizza
Average price: Inexpensive
Area: North Valley/Los Ranchos
Address: 6261 Riverside Plaza Ln
Albuquerque, NM 87120
Phone: (505) 897-1777

#414
Twisters Burgers and Burritos
Cuisines: Mexican, Burgers, Fast Food
Average price: Inexpensive
Area: Midtown/University
Address: 2103 Menaul Blvd NE
Albuquerque, NM 87198
Phone: (505) 884-1828

#415
Freddy's Frozen Custard & Steakburgers
Cuisines: Burgers
Average price: Inexpensive
Area: Eastside
Address: 10201 Central Ave Ne
Albuquerque, NM 87123
Phone: (505) 237-9605

#416
Arturo's Mexican Food
Cuisines: Mexican
Average price: Inexpensive
Area: International District
Address: 325 Louisiana Blvd SE
Albuquerque, NM 87108
Phone: (505) 266-0109

#417
Mac's Steak in the Rough
Cuisines: Fast Food, Mexican, American
Average price: Inexpensive
Area: Midtown/University
Address: 4515 Menaul Blvd NE
Albuquerque, NM 87110
Phone: (505) 888-3611

#418
Ming Dynasty
Cuisines: Chinese
Average price: Inexpensive
Area: Eastside
Address: 1551 Eubank Blvd NE
Albuquerque, NM 87112
Phone: (505) 296-0298

#419
O'Niell's
Cuisines: Sandwiches, Irish Pub, American
Average price: Modest
Area: Nob Hill
Address: 4310 Central Ave SE
Albuquerque, NM 87108
Phone: (505) 255-6782

#420
Hayashi Japanese Steakhouse
Cuisines: Japanese, Sushi Bar, Steakhouse
Average price: Modest
Area: Business Parkway/Academy Acres
Address: 6321 San Mateo Blvd NE
Albuquerque, NM 87109
Phone: (505) 884-0694

#421
Sushi King & Noodles
Cuisines: Sushi Bar, Noodles
Average price: Modest
Area: Downtown
Address: 118 Central Ave SW
Albuquerque, NM 87102
Phone: (505) 842-5099

#422
Weekdays II
Cuisines: Breakfast & Brunch, American
Average price: Inexpensive
Area: Business Parkway/Academy Acres
Address: 4400 Masthead St
Albuquerque, NM 87109
Phone: (505) 821-1731

#423
Which Wich
Cuisines: Sandwiches
Average price: Inexpensive
Area: Business Parkway/Academy Acres
Address: 8110 Louisiana Blvd NE
Albuquerque, NM 87113
Phone: (505) 856-1617

#424
Village Pizza
Cuisines: Pizza
Average price: Inexpensive
Area: North Valley/Los Ranchos
Address: 3851 Rio Grande Blvd
Albuquerque, NM 87107
Phone: (505) 345-9542

#425
Amadeo's Pizza & Subs
Cuisines: Pizza, Salad, Sandwiches
Average price: Inexpensive
Area: Business Parkway/Academy Acres
Address: 585 Osuna Rd NE
Albuquerque, NM 87113
Phone: (505) 344-5555

#426
Yanni's Lemoni Lounge
Cuisines: Greek, Mediterranean, Lounge
Average price: Modest
Area: Nob Hill
Address: 3109 Central Ave NE
Albuquerque, NM 87106
Phone: (505) 268-9250

#427
The Quarters BBQ
Cuisines: Barbeque
Average price: Modest
Area: Airport/Base
Address: 801 Yale Blvd SE
Albuquerque, NM 87106
Phone: (505) 843-6949

#428
Hacienda Del Rio
Cuisines: Mexican
Average price: Modest
Area: Old Town
Address: 302 San Felipe NW
Albuquerque, NM 87104
Phone: (505) 243-3131

#429
Mr Tokyo
Cuisines: Japanese
Average price: Modest
Area: Eastside
Address: 11200 Montgomery Blvd NE
Albuquerque, NM 87111
Phone: (505) 292-4728

#430
Cafe Da Lat
Cuisines: Vietnamese
Average price: Inexpensive
Area: International District
Address: 5615 Central Ave NE
Albuquerque, NM 87108
Phone: (505) 266-5559

#431
Griffs Burger Bar
Cuisines: Burgers, Fast Food
Average price: Inexpensive
Area: International District
Address: 8516 Central Ave SE
Albuquerque, NM 87108
Phone: (505) 255-6130

#432
Sharon's Gourmet To Go
Cuisines: Caterer, Desserts,
Breakfast & Brunch
Average price: Modest
Area: Midtown/University
Address: 3400 Constitution NE
Albuquerque, NM 87106
Phone: (505) 880-0057

#433
El Taco Tote
Cuisines: Mexican
Average price: Inexpensive
Area: Midtown/University
Address: 4701 Central Ave NE
Albuquerque, NM 87108
Phone: (505) 265-5188

#434
JC's New York Pizza Dept
Cuisines: Pizza, Italian
Average price: Inexpensive
Area: Downtown
Address: 215 Central Ave NW
Albuquerque, NM 87102
Phone: (505) 766-6973

#435
O'Niell's
Cuisines: Irish, Pub, American
Average price: Modest
Area: Eastside
Address: 3301 Juan Tabo Blvd NE
Albuquerque, NM 87111
Phone: (505) 293-1122

#436
Genghis Grill
Cuisines: Mongolian
Average price: Modest
Area: Business Parkway/Academy Acres
Address: 4410 The 25 Way NE
Albuquerque, NM 87109
Phone: (505) 344-9335

#437
Pizzeria Luca
Cuisines: Pizza
Average price: Modest
Area: Eastside
Address: 8850 Holly Ave NE
Albuquerque, NM 87122
Phone: (505) 797-8086

#438
ABQ Grill
Cuisines: American
Average price: Modest
Area: Uptown
Address: 2600 Louisiana Blvd NE
Albuquerque, NM 87110
Phone: (505) 881-0000

#439
Scarpas 2
Cuisines: Italian, Pizza, American
Average price: Modest
Area: Eastside
Address: 9700 Montgomery Blvd NE
Albuquerque, NM 87111
Phone: (505) 323-0222

#440
Spinns Burger & Beer
Cuisines: Burgers, American
Average price: Modest
Area: Westside
Address: 4411 Montano Rd NW Ste A
Albuquerque, NM 87120
Phone: (505) 899-6180

#441
Flying Star Cafe
Cuisines: Bakery, American,
Breakfast & Brunch
Average price: Modest
Area: Eastside
Address: 4501 Juan Tabo NE
Albuquerque, NM 87111
Phone: (505) 275-8311

#442
El Sarape
Cuisines: Mexican
Average price: Inexpensive
Area: Midtown/University
Address: 5025 Central Ave NE
Albuquerque, NM 87108
Phone: (505) 266-1907

#443
Cafe Trang
Cuisines: Vietnamese
Average price: Inexpensive
Area: International District
Address: 230 Louisiana Blvd SE
Albuquerque, NM 87108
Phone: (505) 232-6764

#444
Bravo Cucina Italiana
Cuisines: Italian, Gluten-Free, Bar
Average price: Modest
Area: Uptown
Address: 2220 Louisiana Blvd NE
Albuquerque, NM 87110
Phone: (505) 888-1111

#445
Bandido Hideout
Cuisines: Mexican, Gluten-Free, Desserts
Average price: Inexpensive
Area: Midtown/University
Address: 2128 Central Ave SE
Albuquerque, NM 87106
Phone: (505) 242-5366

#446
Stufy's Restaurants
Cuisines: Mexican
Average price: Inexpensive
Area: Eastside
Address: 1311 Juan Tabo Blvd NE
Albuquerque, NM 87112
Phone: (505) 299-1860

#447
Buca di Beppo Italian Restaurant
Cuisines: Italian, Pizza
Average price: Modest
Area: Uptown
Address: 6520 Americas Pkwy NE
Albuquerque, NM 87110
Phone: (505) 872-2822

#448
Stufy's Drive-Thru
Cuisines: Mexican
Average price: Inexpensive
Area: North Valley/Los Ranchos
Address: 1107 Candelaria Rd NW
Albuquerque, NM 87107
Phone: (505) 344-1207

#449
Whole Hog Cafe
Cuisines: Barbeque
Average price: Modest
Area: Downtown
Address: 725 Central Ave NE
Albuquerque, NM 87102
Phone: (505) 247-0189

#450
Annapurna's World Vegetarian Cafe
Cuisines: Vegan, Vegetarian, Gluten-Free
Average price: Modest
Area: Midtown/University
Address: 2201 Silver St SE
Albuquerque, NM 87106
Phone: (505) 262-2424

#451
The Melting Pot
Cuisines: Fondue, Salad
Average price: Expensive
Area: Uptown
Address: 2201 Uptown Lp Rd NE
Albuquerque, NM 87110
Phone: (505) 843-6358

#452
Dion's
Cuisines: Pizza, Sandwiches, Salad
Average price: Inexpensive
Area: Westside
Address: 4200 Montano Rd NW
Albuquerque, NM 87120
Phone: (505) 898-1161

#453
Whataburger
Cuisines: Burgers, Fast Food, American
Average price: Inexpensive
Area: North Valley/Los Ranchos
Address: 200 Menaul NW
Albuquerque, NM 87107
Phone: (505) 242-3876

#454
Scarpas
Cuisines: Italian, Pizza
Average price: Modest
Area: Business Parkway/Academy Acres
Address: 5500 Academy Rd NE
Albuquerque, NM 87109
Phone: (505) 821-1885

#455
Pars Cuisine
Cuisines: Persian/Iranian, Mediterranean
Average price: Modest
Area: Business Parkway/Academy Acres
Address: 4320 The 25 Way NE
Albuquerque, NM 87109
Phone: (505) 345-5156

#456
Satellite Coffee
Cuisines: Breakfast & Brunch, Sandwiches
Average price: Inexpensive
Area: Midtown/University
Address: 1131 University Blvd. Ne
Albuquerque, NM 87102
Phone: (505) 247-0662

#457
The Library Bar and Grill San Mateo
Cuisines: Sports Bar, American
Average price: Modest
Area: Business Parkway/Academy Acres
Address: 5001 San Mateo Blvd NE
Albuquerque, NM 87109
Phone: (505) 883-3285

#458
Pizza 9
Cuisines: Pizza, Italian
Average price: Modest
Area: International District
Address: 5305 Gibson Blvd SE
Albuquerque, NM 87108
Phone: (505) 366-6463

#459
Rudy's Country Store and BBQ
Cuisines: American, Barbeque
Average price: Modest
Area: North Valley/Los Ranchos
Address: 10136 Coors Blvd NW
Albuquerque, NM 87114
Phone: (505) 890-7113

#460
Flying Star Cafe
Cuisines: American, Bakery,
Breakfast & Brunch
Average price: Modest
Area: Uptown
Address: 8001 Menaul Blvd NE
Albuquerque, NM 87110
Phone: (505) 293-6911

#461
Da Vinci's Gourmet Pizza
Cuisines: Pizza
Average price: Modest
Area: Midtown/University
Address: 2904 Indian School NE
Albuquerque, NM 87106
Phone: (505) 275-2722

#462
Piatanzi
Cuisines: Italian, Seafood, Pizza
Average price: Modest
Area: Eastside
Address: 3305 Juan Tabo Blvd NE
Albuquerque, NM 87111
Phone: (505) 296-2340

#463
La Placita Dining Rooms
Cuisines: Mexican, Diner
Average price: Modest
Area: Old Town
Address: 208 San Felipe St NW
Albuquerque, NM 87104
Phone: (505) 247-2204

#464
Gecko's Bar & Tapas
Cuisines: Tapas Bar, Sandwiches, American
Average price: Modest
Area: Business Parkway/Academy Acres
Address: 5801 Academy Rd NE
Albuquerque, NM 87109
Phone: (505) 821-8291

#465
Mimi's Cafe
Cuisines: Breakfast & Brunch, American
Average price: Modest
Area: Business Parkway/Academy Acres
Address: 4316 The 25 Way NE
Albuquerque, NM 87109
Phone: (505) 341-0300

#466
Sandwich Company On Carlisle
Cuisines: Cafe
Average price: Inexpensive
Area: Business Parkway/Academy Acres
Address: 3100 Carlisle Blvd NE
Albuquerque, NM 87110
Phone: (505) 881-0956

#467
Golden Chopsticks
Cuisines: Chinese
Average price: Modest
Area: Eastside
Address: 12251 Academy Rd NE
Albuquerque, NM 87111
Phone: (505) 275-0888

#468
La familiar Mexican Restaurant
Cuisines: American, Mexican
Average price: Inexpensive
Area: Downtown
Address: 1611 4th St NW
Albuquerque, NM 87102
Phone: (505) 242-9661

#469
Garcia's Kitchen
Cuisines: Mexican
Average price: Inexpensive
Area: Uptown
Address: 2924 San Mateo Blvd NE
Albuquerque, NM 87110
Phone: (505) 888-3488

#470
Chez Axel
Cuisines: French
Average price: Modest
Area: Business Parkway/Academy Acres
Address: 6209 Montgomery Blvd NE
Albuquerque, NM 87109
Phone: (505) 881-8104

#471
Le Peep
Cuisines: Breakfast & Brunch, Burgers
Average price: Modest
Area: Eastside
Address: 11004 Montgomery Blvd NE
Albuquerque, NM 87111
Phone: (505) 888-7002

#472
Leroy's New Mexican Food
Cuisines: Mexican
Average price: Modest
Area: Barelas/South Valley
Address: 1209 Old Coors Dr SW
Albuquerque, NM 87121
Phone: (505) 764-0135

#473
New Dragon
Cuisines: Chinese
Average price: Inexpensive
Area: Barelas/South Valley
Address: 9550 Sage Rd SW
Albuquerque, NM 87121
Phone: (505) 839-8417

#474
Cracker Barrel Old Country Store
Cuisines: Southern, American
Average price: Modest
Area: Business Parkway/Academy Acres
Address: 5200 San Antonio Dr NE
Albuquerque, NM 87109
Phone: (505) 821-8777

#475
Jason's Deli
Cuisines: Deli, Sandwiches, Salad
Average price: Inexpensive
Area: Business Parkway/Academy Acres
Address: 5920 Holly Ave NE
Albuquerque, NM 87113
Phone: (505) 821-7100

#476
Aya's New Asian
Cuisines: Japanese, Sushi Bar
Average price: Modest
Area: Uptown
Address: 8019 Menaul Blvd NE
Albuquerque, NM 87110
Phone: (505) 323-5441

#477
WisePies
Cuisines: Salad, Pizza, Fast Food
Average price: Inexpensive
Area: Business Parkway/Academy Acres
Address: 4545 Alameda Blvd NE
Albuquerque, NM 87113
Phone: (505) 821-5260

#478
Fox & Hound Pub & Grill
Cuisines: American, Sports Bar
Average price: Modest
Area: Business Parkway/Academy Acres
Address: 4301 The 25 Way NE
Albuquerque, NM 87109
Phone: (505) 344-9430

#479
Annie's Soup Kitchen
Cuisines: Soup, Sandwiches
Average price: Inexpensive
Area: Eastside
Address: 3107 Eubank Blvd NE
Albuquerque, NM 87111
Phone: (505) 296-8601

#480
Sizzling Thai
Cuisines: Thai
Average price: Inexpensive
Area: Uptown
Address: 8246 Menaul Blvd
Albuquerque, NM 87110
Phone: (505) 750-7916

#481
Weck's
Cuisines: Breakfast & Brunch
Average price: Inexpensive
Area: Business Parkway/Academy Acres
Address: 6650 Holly Ave NE
Albuquerque, NM 87113
Phone: (505) 821-9816

#482
China Casa
Cuisines: Chinese
Average price: Inexpensive
Area: Westside
Address: 111 Coors Blvd NW
Albuquerque, NM 87121
Phone: (505) 839-7771

#483
Chen's Chinese Restaurant
Cuisines: Chinese, Soup
Average price: Inexpensive
Area: Eastside
Address: 235 Juan Tabo Blvd NE
Albuquerque, NM 87123
Phone: (505) 298-9214

#484
May Cafe
Cuisines: Vietnamese
Average price: Inexpensive
Area: International District
Address: 111 Louisiana Blvd SE
Albuquerque, NM 87108
Phone: (505) 265-4448

#485
Wings Gone Wild
Cuisines: American, Chicken Wings
Average price: Modest
Area: Westside
Address: 101 98th St
Albuquerque, NM 87121
Phone: (505) 836-4622

#486
Forasteros Mexican Food
Cuisines: Mexican
Average price: Inexpensive
Area: Midtown/University
Address: 5016 Lomas Blvd NE
Albuquerque, NM 87110
Phone: (505) 508-1079

#487
El Dorado Bakery
Cuisines: Bakery, Mexican
Average price: Inexpensive
Area: Barelas/South Valley
Address: 2125 Broadway Blvd SE
Albuquerque, NM 87102
Phone: (505) 247-2979

#488
Conchita's Cafe
Cuisines: Breakfast & Brunch,
Sandwiches, Mexican
Average price: Inexpensive
Area: Downtown
Address: 400 Gold Ave SW
Albuquerque, NM 87102
Phone: (505) 339-6774

#489
The Barley Room
Cuisines: American, Sports Bar, Caterer
Average price: Modest
Area: Eastside
Address: 5200 Eubank Blvd NE
Albuquerque, NM 87111
Phone: (505) 332-0800

#490
Sandiago's Mexican Grill
Cuisines: Mexican, Deli
Average price: Modest
Area: Eastside
Address: 40 Tramway Rd NE
Albuquerque, NM 87122
Phone: (505) 856-6692

#491
The Last Call
Cuisines: Mexican, Latin American
Average price: Modest
Area: Downtown
Address: 420 Central Ave SW
Albuquerque, NM 87102
Phone: (505) 300-4911

#492
Pizza 9
Cuisines: Pizza, Italian
Average price: Inexpensive
Area: Downtown
Address: 101 Gold Ave Sw
Albuquerque, NM 87102
Phone: (505) 843-6463

#493
Mykonos Cafe and Taverna
Cuisines: Cafe, Bar
Average price: Modest
Area: Eastside
Address: 5900 Eubank Blvd NE
Albuquerque, NM 87111
Phone: (505) 291-1116

#494
South China
Cuisines: Chinese
Average price: Inexpensive
Area: Eastside
Address: 1502 Wyoming Blvd NE
Albuquerque, NM 87112
Phone: (505) 323-0072

#495
Pi Brewing
Cuisines: Pizza, Italian, Brewery
Average price: Modest
Area: North Valley/Los Ranchos
Address: 9780 Coors Blvd NW
Albuquerque, NM 87114
Phone: (505) 890-9463

#496
Flying Star Cafe
Cuisines: Bakery, American,
Breakfast & Brunch
Average price: Modest
Area: Eastside
Address: 8000 Paseo Del Norte NE
Albuquerque, NM 87122
Phone: (505) 923-4211

#497
California Pizza Kitchen
Cuisines: Pizza, American
Average price: Modest
Area: Uptown
Address: 2241 Q St NE
Albuquerque, NM 87110
Phone: (505) 883-3005

#498
Napoli Coffee
Cuisines: Internet Cafe, Sandwiches
Average price: Inexpensive
Area: Midtown/University
Address: 3035 Menaul Blvd NE
Albuquerque, NM 87107
Phone: (505) 884-5454

#499
The Library Bar and Grill
Cuisines: Bar, American
Average price: Modest
Area: Downtown
Address: 312 Central Ave SW
Albuquerque, NM 87102
Phone: (505) 242-2992

#500
Paleteria La Reina de Michoacan
Cuisines: Desserts, Mexican, Ice Cream
Average price: Inexpensive
Area: North Valley/Los Ranchos
Address: 4501 4th St NW
Albuquerque, NM 87107
Phone: (505) 712-3414